To David & Elaine,

In anticipation of your visit

Merry Christmas

love & Best wishes

Steve, Catherine & Camilla Louise xxx

NORWAY

NOR

Originated and developed by
BATO TOMASEVIC

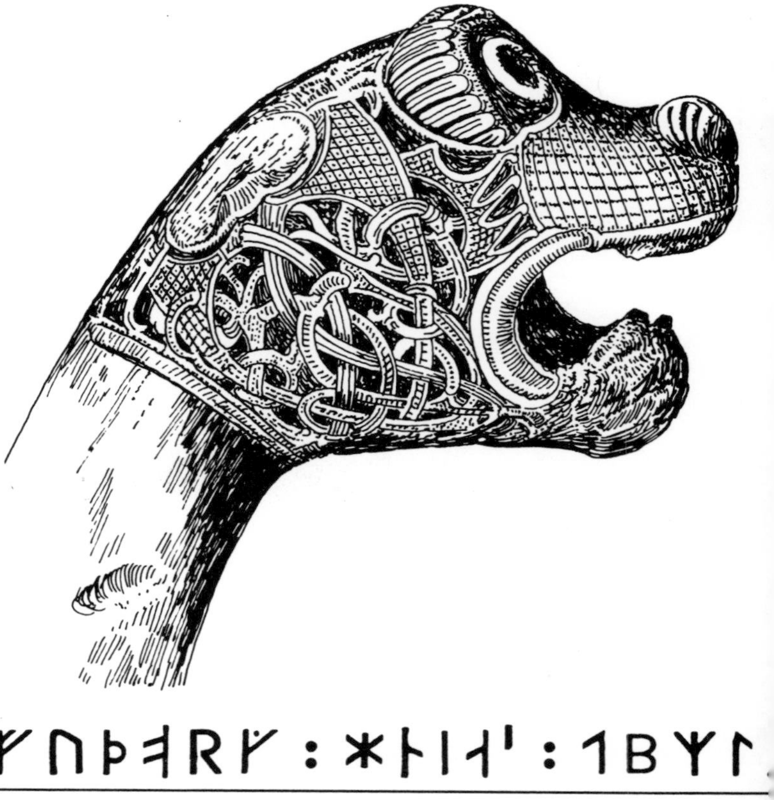

ᚠᚢᚦᚬᚱᚴ : ᚼᚿᛁᛅ' : ᛏᛒᛘᛚ

Text by
GUNVALD OPSTAD

Designed by
GANE ALEKSIC

ASCHEHOUG

A MOTOVUN GROUP BOOK

© H. Aschehoug & Co. (W. Nygaard) / Flint River Press Ltd.

ISBN: 82-03-15447-6

Text by
GUNVALD OPSTAD

Translated by
ANNABELLE DESPARD

Captions by
RAGNAR FRISLID

Printed and bound in Yugoslavia by
DELO, Ljubljana

CONTENTS

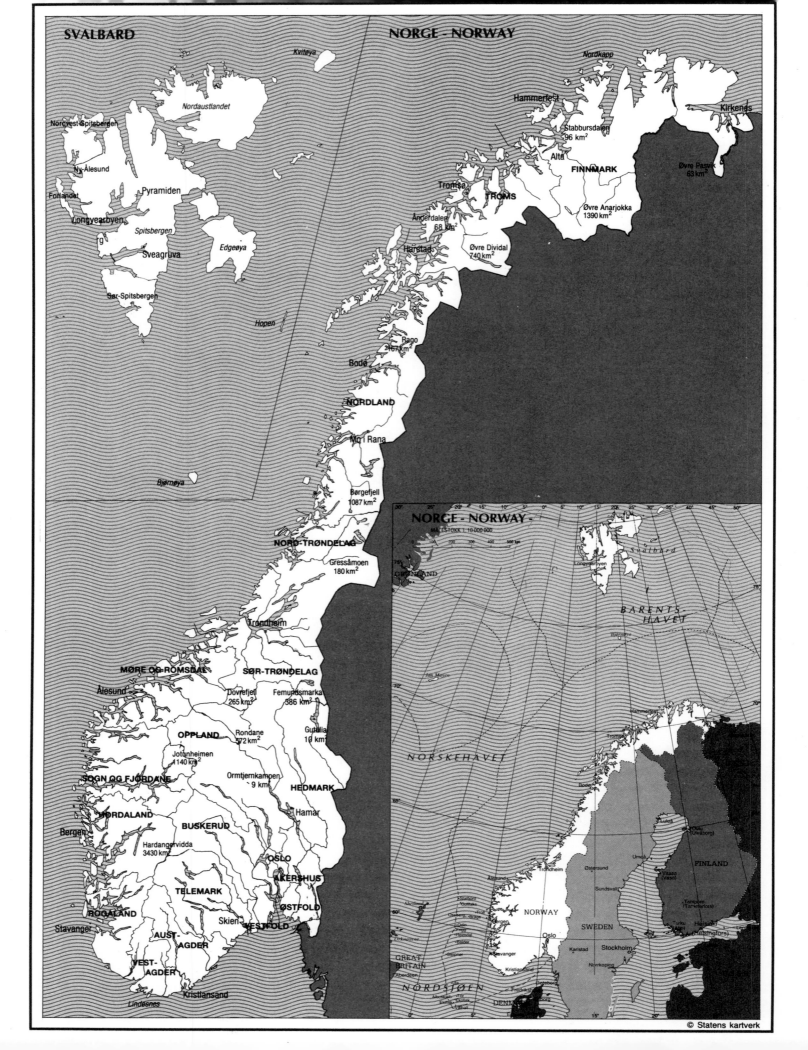

SVALBARD

NORGE - NORWAY

Nordaustlandet

Nordvest-Spitsbergen

Kvitøya

Nordkapp

Hammerfest
Kirkenes

Ny-Ålesund

Stabbursdalen
96 km²

Pyramiden

Alta

Øvre Pasvik
63 km²

Forlandet

FINNMARK

Longyearbyen

Spitsbergen

g

Sveagruva

Edgeøya

Øvre Anarjokka
1390 km²

Sør-Spitsbergen

Tromsø

TROMS

Anderdalen
68 km²

Hopen

Harstad

Øvre Dividal
740 km²

Rago
167 Km²

Bodø

NORDLAND

Mo i Rana

Bjørnøya

Børgefjell
1087 km²

NORD-TRØNDELAG

NORGE - NORWAY

MÅLESTOKK 1:10 000 000

Gressåmoen
180 km²

GRØNLAND

Svalbard

Longyearbyen

BARENTS
HAVET

Bjørnøya

Trondheim

Jan Mayen

MØRE OG ROMSDAL

SØR-TRØNDELAG

NORSKEHAVET

Ålesund

Hammerfest

Dovrefjell
265 km²

Femundsmarka
386 km²

Tromsø

Rondane
572 km²

Gutulia
19 km²

OPPLAND

Jotunheimen
1140 km²

Bodø

Ormtjernkampen
9 km²

SOGN OG FJORDANE

HEDMARK

Trondheim

Østersund

Umeå

FINLAND

Hamar

HORDALAND

Ålesund

Vaasa
(Vasa)

BUSKERUD

Bergen

Sundsvall

Hardangervidda
3430 km²

Tampere
(Tammerfors)

OSLO

NORWAY

Bergen

AKERSHUS

SWEDEN

Turku
(Åbo)

Helsinki
(Helsingfors)

TELEMARK

Oslo

ØSTFOLD

ROGALAND

Skien

VESTFOLD

Karlstad

Stockholm

Stavanger

AUST-
AGDER

Kristiansand

Norrköping

VEST-
AGDER

GREAT
BRITAIN

Kristiansand

Göteborg

Lindesnes

NORDSJØEN

DENM

© Statens kartverk

THE NORWEGIANS

CHAPTER ONE deals with the difficult problem of describing 4,233,116 individuals who live more scattered around than most people in Europe.

Mrs and Mr Typical Norwegian, Kari and Ola Nordmann, who are they? In 1990 there were 4,233,116 different answers to that question. Ola Nordmann is not, of course, that real person living near Oslo who has trouble every time he tries to pay by cheque, because all banks in Norway use his name in their advertisements demonstrating how Ola the Norwegian should fill in a cheque correctly. No, I think of that ordinary, average couple who inhabit this extraordinarily extended piece of land, 1,752 kilometres (1,088 miles) from north to south, but only 6.5 kilometres (4 miles) wide in the middle.

"The people are extremely friendly and helpful. People trust each other entirely, and they never lock their houses. The fishermen build their own boats and make all their tackle," reported the Italian nobleman and merchant Pietro Querini, after being stranded on the island of Røst in Lofoten in the north of Norway in January 1432.

"The Norwegians have fire and temperament and are open, plain-spoken and forthright without being insolent. They never flatter their superiors, but show suitable respect. The normal manner of salutation is to shake hands, and when we gave them or paid them a coin or two, they shook our hands heartily and genuinely, not bowing or putting their thanks into words," wrote the English archdeacon William Coxe, in his travel journal in 1784.

"A general slowness and a fondness for bad food are the only poor qualities we have detected in the Norwegian. He is, for example, ridiculously honest, and he is kind and hospitable," wrote the Englishmen J. A. Lees and W. J. Clutterbuck, in their travelogue *Three in Norway by Two of Them* in 1882.

"The Norwegian is by nature (compared with Frisian smallholders) introverted and reserved, slow in thinking and in action, and in addition suspicious of strangers. Therefore: do not be hasty. Take things calmly." Thus Hitler exhorted the German troops who were to occupy Norway in 1940.

"Norwegians are so unsophisticated, refreshing, open and warm," said the violinist Iona Brown, Artistic Director of the Academy of St Martin-in-the-Fields chamber orchestra, in 1986.

"You are so one-track minded. All Norwegians think alike and talk about the same things: work and money, drinking and their·next holiday,'' said a Yugoslav in 1987 after having stayed in Norway for a long time.

True – all too true!

In addition to the fact that 50 murders are committed in Norway each year, that 100,000 Norwegians are so harassed at work that 100 of them commit suicide annually, that 400,000 people get stomach ulcers in the course of their lives, that 400,000 get diarrhoea each year because of impurities in the drinking water, that there are 100,000 in hospital queues, that hospitals are closed because of lack of funds, that care for the elderly is so poor that even 101-year-olds are sent home, that two billion kroner is paid out in social benefits per year, that 25,000 people need social benefits in Oslo alone, that 7,000 a year are arrested for drug abuse, 100 people die of an overdose, and around 500 prostitute themselves to get drugs, that one billion is lost in thefts from shops, that tax evasion and insurance swindles each amounts to 15 billion, that 60,000 cars are stolen or broken into and there is no guarantee that you can report the crime immediately as telephone booths are vandalized to the tune of 25 million kroner per year. (100 kroner = c. $ 1.50 or £ 0.90 in 1991.)

All this has to be mentioned at this early stage to give a balanced picture.

Ola Nordmann could be that man standing shivering on Karl Johan, Oslo's main street, with frost in his beard and a drip under his nose, staring blindly at beaches, palms and glittering sunlight on the travel agent's Florida poster. Kari Nordmann could well be that liberated topless woman who lies in glittering sunlight on Sjøsanden beach in Mandal, suntanned and carefree, while her child plays in the sand. Ola Nordmann could equally be the Såmi (Lapp) on his snowscooter on Finnmarksvidda, for Norway is also the Såmiland (Lappland). Or he could belong to the number of travellers, tinkers and gypsies who have lived among us with their own language for many hundreds of years. It is, in fact, quite an undertaking to explain what Norway is and what Norwegians are.

Yet if we are to draw up some common characteristics, it would be these: Norwegians do not march in step like the Germans, nor do they move in flocks like the Japanese, but they go about singly like goats. They have vast expanses of country on all sides to wander around in, and what exciting and varied country it is! Norwegians have more breathing space than most: there are 13 people to each square kilometre in Norway, while there are 89 in Yugoslavia, 100 in France, 228 in Great Britain, and 18,121 in Monaco!

Yet while Kari and Ola are born with the proverbial skis on and grow up with rucksacks on their backs, they have fully surrendered to the Anglo-American influence that assails them day and night. This makes them a confused mixture of country bumpkin and wordly-wise, one foot in the potato-patch and the other on the aircraft steps – and may heaven help them from doing the splits.

After all, it's not as if they hadn't been abroad before; in fact, as long ago as the Viking age. Norway claims to have 'discovered' America, as Europeans so arrogantly say of lands whose peoples, in their innocence, were never aware of being discovered. In 1964 President Lyndon B. Johnson proclaimed 9 October an official flagday throughout the U.S.A. in honour of Leif Eriksson. The only trace of him is to be seen in the foundations of some dwellings in Newfoundland and Leif Eriksson

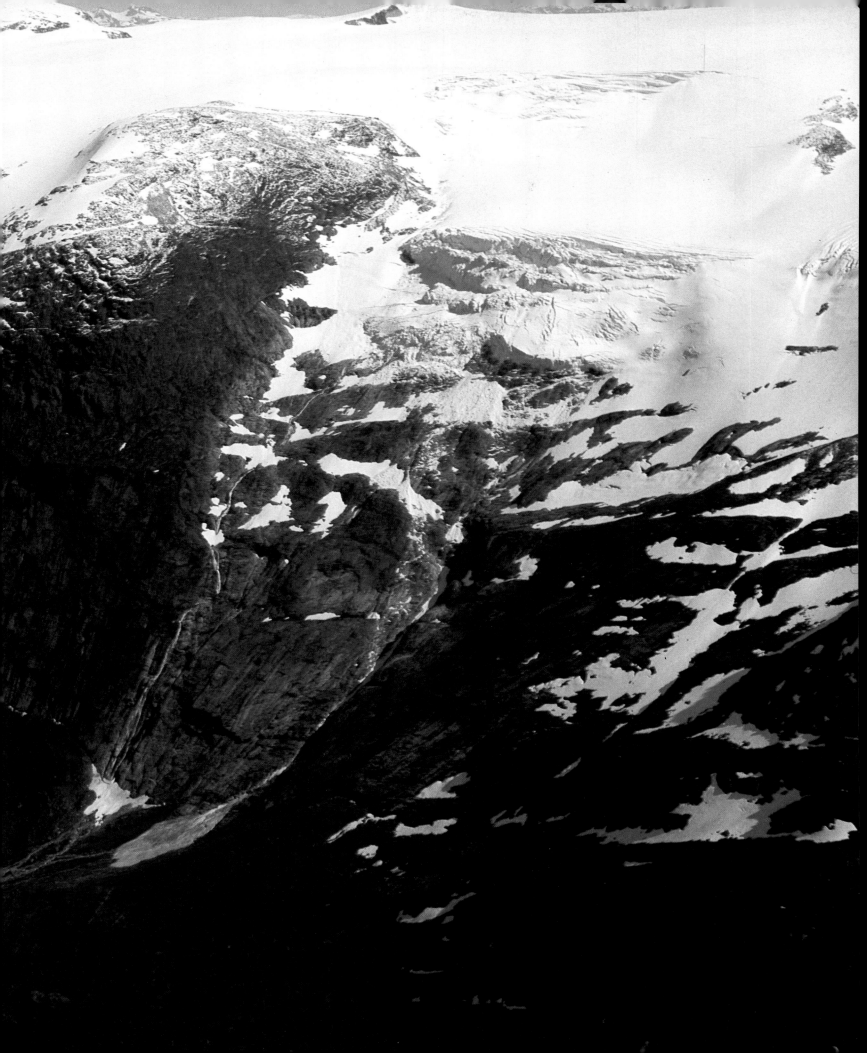

4

4. Salmon farming has become a new industry, and one fish farm gives way to the next all along the coast. This picture is from Svolvær. (Husmo-Foto)

5. While the Lofoten mountains are still covered by snow, the cod come in to spawn and the fishing fleet goes out to meet them. (Husmo-Foto) ▷

6. A lonely ski-track stretching across a wintery mountain landscape, with sparkling sun and deep shadows, is the dream of many a Norwegian. This picture is from the Bergen mountains in the county of Hordaland. (Helge Sunde) ▷ ▷

7. The Scandinavian reindeer (Rangifer tarandus) has long been domesticated by the Såmi (Lapps), but herds still roam wild in southern parts of Norway, feeding mostly on 'reindeer moss' and other species of lichen. Its North American cousin is the caribou. (Hans Hvide Bang/Samfoto/NN) ▷ ▷ ▷

8. Swimming across the sound to the island of Magerøya, herds of reindeer have sometimes perished in storms. Nowadays, the Norwegian Navy usually ferries the animals across to their summer pastures. (Hans Hvide Bang/Samfoto/NN) ▷ ▷ ▷ ▷

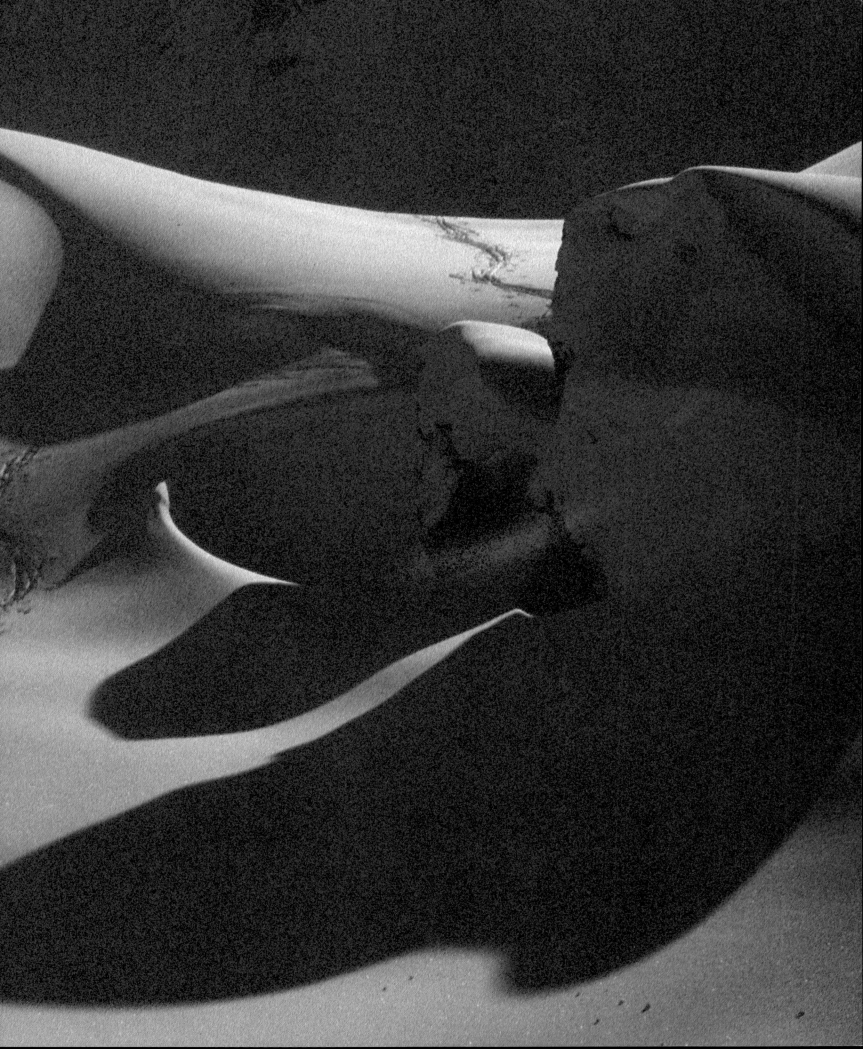

Drive in Brooklyn. Amerigo Vespucci, who arrived 500 years later, had the entire continent named after him. This should really have been called South Eriksson and North Eriksson! But that's how things are for explorers from the provinces. Norway can, however, boast a large piece of Antarctic ice that is called Queen Maud Land, after a Norwegian queen.

Thor Heyerdahl never staked a claim to Easter Island; nor Liv Ullman to the Mid-West, which she conquered in Jan Troell's epic film on the Scandinavian emigration to the U.S.A. However, in the telephone directory in Minneapolis, Minnesota, there are 10 pages of Olsons. And Olson is the son of Ola Nordmann.

Despite their small number and out-of-the-way country, there are occasions when Norwegians have unshakeable confidence that they are the best. How else to explain their fervent missionary activity? In proportion to the size of its population, Norway has more missionaries than any other country in the world. In 1987, 1,369 of them were sent out to 56 different countries! Most of these are paid for by voluntary contributions through organizations such as the Norwegian Mission Society, founded in 1842. At the Annual General Meeting in 1987 it was said that the missionary's territory is no longer south of the Equator. Now it is Europe's turn to be brought to Christianity. The first Norwegian missionaries have already been sent to France, and after that Portugal, Italy and Austria lie open to them.

Norway is reckoned to be the most puritan of the Scandinavian countries. Ninety per cent of the population belongs to the State Church, established at the Reformation in 1536, but only 37 per cent open their Bibles in the course of the year. There are 600 free congregations with 150,000 members in Norway, 18,000 Catholics, and 8,000 Muslims.

A Norwegian is by nature shy, and modesty is also a characteristic of the country's non-Christian population. In the eyes of Americans and Southern Europeans, the whole of Scandinavia is collectively an exponent of Swedish sin. Yet pornography has never been legal in Norway, and has never been sold openly, as in Sweden and Denmark. What goes on under the counter is a different story. To do things furtively is more in accordance with our nature. When Ola Nordmann needed to buy rubber contraceptives in the 60s, he discreetly placed two fingers on the counter at the barber's, and while he modestly kept his glance averted, the barber stooped to look into his drawer and brought out the much-needed two dozen. Today condoms are available in 2,500 shops, in supermarkets and at petrol stations. Accessibility follows geographical patterns of morality. It is easiest to buy condoms in Akershus, near Oslo, and in the north, most difficult in the west and south.

In the 60s it was shameful to produce a child out of wedlock in Norway. Up to 1973 common law marriage was illegal. However, it seems that this ruling slept more soundly than the couples themselves, for out of the 50,000 children born each year in Norway, one in four is born out of wedlock. In Finnmark every second child has unmarried parents, and in Oslo every third. This does not mean that Norwegians are much less moral than in earlier years; they have merely found another way of life. In 1986 70,000 were registered as co-habiting without being married, and the real figures must be much higher. In 1970 15 per cent of the population consisted of single persons, today it is 40 per cent. Around the turn of the century each family comprised on average 4.3 persons; today it is 2.5. Kari gives birth to an average 1.7 children, too few to keep up the population. In the north the population is already

9. Where fjords block the advance of motorists, car ferries take over, as here in Geiranger fjord.
(Husmo-Foto)

strongly on the decline, while the figures show an increase in the east and in the 'oil counties' of west Norway. To counteract this we are living longer. Life expectancy today is 80 years for women and 73 for men. We are also growing. The average Norwegian recruit to the armed services towers 1.79 metres (5 ft. 10 inches) above sea level, the tallest ever.

How do Kari and Ola live?

The answer is very well indeed. The houses are so thoroughly insulated that experts are becoming concerned at the possible dangers of not letting air in! Kari and Ola like to live by themselves, in their own small nuclear unit, without any interference from the rest of the family. Grandma is placed in a home — if there is room for her. This is one of the most surprising things to foreigners. Care for the aged is a major unsolved problem of the welfare state. Out of the country's 1.5 million private dwellings, 640,000 are detached houses, 275,000 are flats, 160,000 farms, 160,000 terraced houses, and 70,000 are semi-detached. But as mortgages and bank rates soar out of all proportion, it is increasingly difficult to buy a home, especially for the young. Many Norwegians simply cannot pay their rent, and some 80,000 receive housing benefits from the State.

Norwegians are obsessed by furniture. Everyone spends on average 1,500 kroner per year on furniture, while Europeans in 15 other countries spend a mere third of this amount. Much of it is IKEA i.e. make-it-yourself furniture from the Swedish mail order firm that each year prints 44 million catalogues in 10 languages for 18 countries. Foreigners are amazed at the amount of furniture Norwegians manage to cram into their houses. Though the government appeals to the population to reduce consumption, Mr and Mrs Nordmann just go on spending: on freezers and washing-machines, tumbledriers and microwave ovens, stereos and CD equipment.

There are now 1.9 million cars on the roads. This means 2.5 persons per car in Norway, compared with 2.2 in West Germany and 1.4 in the USA. There are 200,000 Fords and Opels in the country, 150,000 VWs and Volvos, but only 40 Rolls-Royces and 32 Packards, one Bombardier and one Büssing, whatever that might be.

Many people own cabins and have pleasure craft that cost almost as much as a house. So there is plenty of money around. The level of spending is high, and the consumer mentality is spreading, not least among the younger generation. Young people of today, between the ages of eight and 24, spend an average 1,000 kroner a month on themselves. This can easily be seen by looking in the mail box. Nowhere is superfluous consumption as apparent as there! Every day the poor Norwegian has to empty his mail box of wads of leaflets advertising everything from package tours to magnet rings against hay fever, from sentimental novels to courses in Advanced Yoga. Each year the Post Office delivers 550 million commercial offers, with or without an address. Each household receives 320 of these missives in the course of a year. In addition there will be as many from the local store or local organizations. If Kari and Ola co-habit and have different family names, they will receive double the amount of junk mail. No wonder they have taken out bank loans for up to 250 billion kroner to make ends meet. It is poor consolation to know that they can deduct 30 billion kroner in interest off their income tax.

If they are not satisfied with what they have bought, they can complain to the consumer's Ombudsman. He has offices throughout the country, and received 130,000 complaints in 1986. Children can register complaints with the Ombudsman for children, while matters of sexual discrimination can go to the equal rights Ombudsman. Life in Norway is highly regulated. This is seen as a blessing in a welfare state, the expression of a healthy social democratic concern for one's fellow men, even if the rules do become somewhat bureaucratic at times.

Norway is fairly broad-minded as far as animal rights go, permitting both battery hens and pork factories, with the pigs eating and mating on demand as well as artificially. Yet in many high-rise flats it is forbidden to keep pets. With our strongly developed sense of hygiene, we never cease to wonder at the pigs and hens let loose in villages in more southerly climates.

We do, however, accept animals as symbols. They are acceptable at a distance. Swamped as we are in Walt Disney fauna, it is surely an acceptable face of nationalism to start looking for what is essentially Norwegian in our animal kingdom. The State Radio asked the people to proclaim the National Fish, whereupon one group of wits lobbied for the hagfish, an eel that most people would vote the most repulsive form of marine life. Needless to say, the State Radio made sure that the title went to the cod. It is hardly elevating to remember the choice of the dipper as the National Bird. It is now in danger of being made extinct by acid rain from England and the Continent, a fate that also threatens fish in all the lakes in southern Norway.

Recently a considerable effort has been made to have the small Norwegian pony proclaimed National Animal. This horse came from the steppes of Russia some 4,000 years ago, and has worked very hard as a packhorse in the west of Norway and in the timber forests of eastern Norway. Good-natured, modest in its demands, with short legs and a happy disposition, it has become a favourite in Norwegian children's songs. But it too, alas, is in danger of dying out. A generation ago we had 70,000 *Fjordings* or Norwegian ponies, today there are only 5,000 left. Friends of the Fjording want it to replace the lion on the Norwegian coat of arms!

It seems that it is in his diet that the Norwegian has succumbed most to foreign influence in recent years. Cafés have traditionally been small dour rooms with plastic table-tops, metal chairs, and silent people, serving neither beer nor spirits, only tired cheese sandwiches, bland stew, fish balls or meat loaf with stewed cabbage and boiled potatoes – and all closing at five in the afternoon. Nowadays, the main items on the diet of those under 30 are potato crisps and Coke, and there are trendy cafés everywhere with marble table-tops and rock music, pizzas and pasta, hamburgers and cappuchino. All this compelled Ragnvald Hidle from the puritan Jæren district to sit down and write to his newspaper in the oil town Stavanger:

"We live in strange times when all things foreign and weird are made out to be so wonderful. Foreign names and foreign fancy food enjoy an exaggerated reputation. Perhaps there is reason to ask as Henrik Ibsen did: 'Is the greatest then so great?' There are many of us who cannot get to good teetotal places where we can buy good plain Norwegian country fare: porridge, dumplings, meat balls, *lefse*, waffles, pancakes and decent bread rolls. We should get together and start a decent old-fashioned *matstove*, a café for those who care about dialect preservation, the Bible Society, clean-living young people and others . . . ''

That I would call a true Norwegian sentiment! But what is Norwegian and what is not Norwegian in the realm?

The national musical instrument is the harding fiddle, but young people listen to 'A-Ha', the Norwegian pop group that topped charts all over the world in the 80s — singing in English! Yet a Norwegian swells with pride when he sees members of the group wearing the true, all-Norwegian hand-knitted Setesdal sweater. Cod-liver oil is Norwegian, lurking in the fridge as a terror to all children, part of the staple diet for 130 years. Reindeer horn is also Norwegian, ground for medical purposes, but strangely enough used more as an aphrodisiac in the Far East than in Norway.

Then there is *smalahove*, a singed sheep's head that smiles up at you from its plate, which is the traditional festive dish of the west. We shall refrain from saying too much about this, out of consideration for the nation's good name and reputation. We shall return to the dried fish later, also to aquavit.

Our aim with this book is to follow Kari and Ola through history, through their lives, through the seasons, through the country. Let us hasten to bring to your notice yet another Norwegian phenomenon before others do so: the duvet, or *dyne*. That too has a long tradition. As early as 1799 the French officer Jacques-Louis de Bougrenet de la Tocnaye wrote in his journal *Promenade en Norvège*:

"In Sweden one is seldom given more than a light cotton blanket as a covering, even in winter. In this country one buries oneself in a huge eiderdown, even in summer. I for my part cannot keep this over me for more than a quarter of an hour without being bathed in sweat."

Nordmanns forbundet, or the Norseman Federation has members all over the world. The General Secretary Johan Fr. Heyerdahl tells us what genuinely Norwegian things Norwegian-Americans want sent over.

"I have sent many stones and pieces of rock over the pond to those who wished to have a piece of Norwegian granite in the foundations of their house. And duvets. Norwegian-Americans cannot do without them once they have tried them on a visit to Norway..."

Norwegians are very kind — at a distance. As a country we hold the world record in giving aid to developing countries. Yet it is a different story when we are asked to receive refugees from Iran and Sri Lanka. The General Secretary of *Nordmanns forbundet* has a comment on this:

"We need all the inspiration we can get from outside in this small country of ours. I feel there is an alarming attitude of 'Go it alone'. What has created this fear of other countries, cultures and customs, of foreign influences? Just look at our lack of hospitality! We have a lot to learn from the Americans. In the U.S.A. you are invited to have a cup of coffee — and you get a cup of coffee. Getting to know each other is the essential thing."

Just to get some things straight:

Some foreigners wonder about the 'houses' they see beside Norwegian roads. They look like log cabins, but they are very low and have no windows. Do not expect to be invited in. These are woodpiles, layers of logs that will give warmth through the long winter nights when we live up to the ideal of hospitality described in our first book of etiquette *Håvamål* that goes back nearly a thousand years:

"Fire he needs who has come in cold about the knee."

They certainly needed some warmth about the knee, those first people who came to this bleak country.

HISTORY

CHAPTER TWO tells about how the first Norsemen settled next to the icecap, sailed off course and 'discovered' America, but decided to return home and become Social Democrats.

The first settlers probably arrived 10,000 to 11,000 years ago, and they must have been tough. How else could they have come to Norway? Northern Europe has been covered by ice four times in the course of the past million years, and the last ice age was then in retreat. They came to the foot of the glacier, in hide boats and hollowed-out tree trunks, driven by curiosity, or perhaps chased from their homelands. Some may have come overland. A bare strip of land is thought to have remained in both the south and north of Norway throughout the last ice age, and there are experts who believe that a tribe could have survived the long winter there, living like the Eskimos have done until recent times.

Some settled in the south, others in the north. Scientists cannot agree as to who came first; it seems that archaeologists are as regionally biased as anybody else. One site found near the Oslo fjord is assumed to date back 10,000 years. But the richest finds are in the west and north of Norway. These nomadic hunters made their first tools of antler and bone. In his history of Norway, Professor Andreas Holmsen reflects on the uses of these tools:

''(They) fully covered the needs of primitive people. They could make boats of wood and hide and row among the skerries and islands, they could shoot seals and whales with their excellent bone harpoons, and they could fish with hooks or spears of bone. Inland they could kill game, such as reindeer, moose, deer, bears and wild horses, with bows and arrows or with javelins. On the seashore they could gather shellfish with their bare hands, and we know that they had ways of catching sea birds and animals without any implements at all.''

Holmsen goes on to describe how these small groups of fishermen and hunters lived their lives, independent of the outside world, and on the whole independent of one another. Yet it does not mean that they were not in touch, or closed to external influences, which would necessarily have come from the east, since they had not yet set out to sea westwards.

After 5,000 years the Norseman started to till the soil and keep domestic animals. He was then visited by warring Indo-European invaders who poured into Europe at that time. It is thought that this led to the development of some form of warrior class. After all, the Vikings must have got their ferocious nature from somewhere.

By A.D. 700 they were fully fledged and raring to go. The homestead and the clan were by now well established, and society was properly divided into masters and serfs, as shown by the medieval Frostating Law, which states that he who pokes out the eyes of another shall pay a fine of a farm and 12 head of cattle, two horses and two slaves. By now neighbourhood feuds were the accepted pastime and passion, the Viking ships had been invented, and general fury was at boiling-point.

They were now ready and could overcome half Europe, invade Ireland and take on England (though it was actually the Danes who did that), they could found Russia (or was it a Swede who did that?) and they could discover America (that we do know was a Norwegian, even if in his heart he was perhaps Icelandic or a Greenlander). When it comes to claiming great deeds we have elastic notions of nationality.

What drove them to this? What makes people abandon hearth and home, concubines and swine, in order to court the dangers of the unknown, drink themselves into a frenzy, rape, loot and pillage, and generally make themselves at home in another land?

It seems there were three reasons:
1) They had killed someone and needed to flee.
2) They had no clue as to where they were sailing.
3) They were bored.

All this emerges clearly from the saga of the discovery of America. It is well known that Leif Eriksson discovered America (though in all truth another man got there first, the Viking Bjarne Herjolvsson, but he couldn't be bothered to step ashore!).

Leif Eriksson's father was a Norseman, Eric the Red, who had had to flee Norway because he had killed a man. He went to Iceland, where he committed more murders and had to move further west on the island. There he had a major dispute with a neighbour who had borrowed some timber from him, which led to his being outlawed, and going over the sea to the larger island further west again.

Leif Eriksson's father never reached America, but it is quite clear that he was the founder of the modern American advertising business. According to the saga: "He called the country he had found Greenland, as he said it would make people want to travel there if the country had a good name."

Leif Eriksson, the discoverer of America, had actually aimed to go to Greenland. He had been home to Norway on a visit and had taken on the task of converting Greenland to Christianity for the king of Norway, Olav Tryggvason.

The Vinland Saga relates:

"Now Leif put out to sea and he sailed for a long time and found land that he did not know before. There, there were wheatfields which were self-sown, and wine-trees grew there. There were trees which are called *massur*, and of all these things they collected samples."

Leif had a half-sister, Frøydis, and she later visited Vinland with her brothers Helge and Finnboge, who had just come from Norway. This description of their visit to Leif's huts in Newfoundland provides definite proof that boredom was the mainspring of Viking violence:

"Now winter came and the brothers spoke about playing games in order to pass the time, and this they did until they started quarrelling.

then they gave up the games and did not visit each other, and so things went on for some time.''

It ended with Frøydis having every man in the next house killed, including her own brothers:

''Thus the men were slain but the women were left, and nobody would kill them. Then said Frøydis, 'Let me have an axe'. So it was done, and she struck at the five women, and did not leave off until they were all dead.'' So goes the saga, which also relates how Frøydis promised to kill anyone who told tales once they were back in Greenland. If boredom led to episodes of this kind in a domestic setting, what kind of treatment must have lain in store for total strangers?

In the 1960s, Norwegian archaeologist Anne Stine Ingstad discovered at L'Anse aux Meadows in Newfoundland what are assumed to be the remains of the *Leifsbuene*, or Leif's huts, with a spinning wheel of soapstone and a Viking ornament, a find that is considered one of the most worthy of preservation in the world after the Egyptian Pyramids.

It was around the year 1000 that the natives of Newfoundland, the *Skrælingers* or Weaklings, as the saga calls them, found out the disadvantages of being in the path of the Vikings. Leif's brother Torvald came across the first nine natives, and ''took them all prisoner except one, who got away in his boat. They killed the other eight, and then they went back to the hill and looked about them.'' Another Viking, Torfinn Karlsevne, and his men were sailing homewards and ''on their way they came upon some *Skrælingers* asleep, dressed in skins. They had with them birch-bark sacks containing food and animal bones mixed with blood. Karlsevne and his men concluded they must be outlaws, and killed them.'' That was the way we discovered America.

By 790 the fun had started in Europe. Three Norwegian ships came

Medieval painting showing scenes from the life of St Olav. Drawing by Magnus Petersen.

to England. The king's man rode out to meet them, but in their customary manner the Vikings struck him down. That is all the Anglo-Saxon Chronicle has to relate about the matter. The next attack, on 8 June 793, was on St Cuthbert's monastery at Lindisfarne, the religious centre of Northumberland. The Vikings fell upon the defenceless monks and nuns, killed some of them, drowning a few, slaughtering their cattle and carting the meat on board ship. The honourable saga of the Vikings had started. The rest is well known.

They had already settled on the islands north of Scotland: the Shetland (Hjaltland) and Orkney Isles. From there they moved north to the Faroes and south to northern Scotland (Sudrland) and the Hebrides (Sudrøyene). Anyone who happened to be on the islands was unceremoniously ousted. There are still 100,000 Norse place names in the Shetlands, where the farmers spoke Norwegian right up to the beginning of the nineteenth century!

In the 820s the Irish coastland was full of Vikings. By 850 most of the Celtic region was Norwegian. In the Golden Age of Dublin, around 950, there was a Norwegian king in each district, a Norwegian chieftain in each town, and a Norwegian warrior in each house. On the Isle of Man, a *ting* or assembly is still held each summer at Tynwald according to the old Norwegian custom. This has been an unbroken tradition since 979, and the British monarch or royal representative has to turn up.

The voyages of destruction went south through the rivers of France, round Spain and into the Mediterranean. In France and southern Europe the Norwegian and Danish Vikings operated together, while in Constantinople they met the Swedes, who had arrived there by way of the rivers of Russia. Towards the end of the ninth century the Vikings' grip embraced virtually the whole of Europe.

They wrought havoc on the coastlands around the North Sea, the English Channel and the Bay of Biscay. They held the Frisian Islands, and they sailed up the Elbe and the Rhine. They burnt Hamburg, laid waste to Cologne, Aachen and Koblenz, and forced their way up the River Mosel to Trier. They pitched camp on the estuaries of the Loire and Seine and went on voyages of plunder to Orleans and Paris. In the 880s the Seine was invaded by a Viking fleet so large (700 ships with 40,000 men) that the vessels covered the river for a distance of 20 kilometres (12 miles) from Paris. There was no greater invasion of Europe from the north until the discovery of Majorca by package tourists 1100 years later! The Norsemen made their way to Toulouse and conquered Bordeaux, fought the Moors at Lisbon, and took possession of Seville before they were themselves defeated. They even visited the west coast of Morocco. While in the Mediterranean, they made raids into Africa, Spain and France. All this was in addition to colonizing Iceland and Greenland.

The Viking era lasted from around 800 to 1050. Its greatest influence was in seven places: the kingdoms of Dublin and Man, the earldom of the Orkneys, and the settlements of the Shetlands, Faroes, Iceland and Greenland. In France Normandy got its name from the Norsemen, and the reputation for quarrelsomeness lasted for a long time. When our friend the French officer Jacques de la Tocnaye travelled around Norway 200 years ago, he noted in his journal:

"In latter years the government has tried to stay the passion for litigation that is as characteristic of Norwegians as of their descendants in France. In each town there are now two courts of arbitration where the parties have to meet before their case can be brought to court..."

10. *The impressive Vigeland Sculpture Park is one of Oslo's biggest attractions. It is the work of a single artist: sculptor Gustav Vigeland.* (Pål Hermansen/ Samfoto/NN)

11. *Vigeland Park, which forms part of Frogner Park in Oslo, contains about 190 sculptural works, most depicting human beings and made of bronze or granite.* (Husmo-Foto) ▷

12. *Oslo is a city with its face turned to the sea. The medieval castle of Akershus and the City Hall are familiar landmarks for anyone sailing into the capital.* (Husmo-Foto) ▷ ▷

13. *The sculptures of Vigeland Park show Man in all stages of life, from birth to death.* (M. Løberg/Samfoto/NN)

14. Centrally placed in Vigeland Park
is this monolith which is nearly 17
metres (55 feet) tall. 121 human
figures are carved into this single slab
of stone weighing 250 tons. (Husmo-
Foto)

15. The climax of Constitution Day in Oslo is the children's parade, which ends in front of the Royal Palace, where the king greets the children from the balcony. (Mittet)

16. Nearly every school has its band, and they all practise incessantly in spring, in preparation for the great event – the children's parade on 17 May. (Mittet)

17. Constitution Day, 17 May, with its parades and festivities, may become too much for a small girl. When that happens, father's shoulders are the best resting place, and ensure the best view of what is going on. (Mittet) 17

18. Patient citizens of Oslo lining up for the bus in snowy weather near the city's cathedral. (Husmo-Foto)

19. Though Oslo is a coastal city, its position at the end of a long fjord gives it a continental climate with cold winters and heavy snow. (Husmo-Foto)

20. Thanks to the Gulf Stream, winters are milder along the Norwegian coast than anywhere else on a similar latitude, and winter clouds deposit more rain and sleet than snow. This is the town of Ålesund. (Knut Enstad)

19

21. In front of Oslo City Hall stand statues of the Mason and five other craftsmen, all created by the sculptor Per Palle Storm. (Husmo-Foto)

22, 23. The Viking Ship House at Bygdøy in Oslo displays three vessels, all of them found in burial mounds near Oslo fjord. (Svein-Erik Dahl/ Samfoto)

24. On hot summer days, crowds flock to Vigeland Park, mingling with its 650 sculptural figures. (Husmo-Foto)

25. Open-air cafés and thousands of people fill the pedestrian zone streets of Oslo in summer. (Husmo-Foto)

The Vikings had their own mythology and cosmology, the remains of which can still be found in Norway. We say: "There goes Thor with his hammer" when we hear thunder. The Christian daily paper *Vart Land* has Odin's messengers, the ravens Hugin and Munin, depicted above its satire column, and in the North Sea many of the oil fields and rigs bear names from Viking mythology, such as Valhalla, Balder, Hod, Heidrun, Sleipner.

There is no founder as such of the Norse beliefs, and no set of dogma. However, there is an epic of creation, with the two first human beings, Ash and Alder, and there is the apocalyptic vision of the end of the world, Ragnarok. The world tree, Yggdrasil, was central to the Viking religion, which had much in common with Greek mythology. Thor was the most popular god, riding across the skies, hammer in hand, in his goat-drawn chariot. The one-eyed Odin, god of war, rode the eight-legged horse Sleipnir, and received fallen warriors in Valhalla, where they awoke to new life and new battles. Frøya was the goddess of love, and Iduna the giver of eternal youth. The home of the gods, the Aesir, was in Asgard. The humans dwelt in Midgard while the giants, the Jotuns, lived in Utgard, the wild country of Jotunheimen (the present name of Norway's central mountain range).

A strong streak of fatalism permeated the Viking outlook and also their superstition, their belief in elves and fates, goblins and trolls. All these are found in Norwegian folk tales. People still believed in trolls and supernatural beings until the recent past.

Historians tell us not to judge our ancestors by our own standards, but by theirs. So we will be careful of labelling our hero kings murderers, torturers, and arsonists. Yet it was no straight-forward matter when the old Viking kings made up their minds to introduce their subjects to the gentle teachings of Jesus, the 'White Christ' as they called him.

One of the men who converted Norway to Christianity was Olav Tryggvason, perhaps the most fabled king in Norway's history, 'the most beautiful, the greatest and strongest and the most widely renowned athlete of all Norsemen', according to Snorre Sturlason, writer of the Icelandic Prose Saga. King Olav's special prowess was running on the oars of a ship outside the hull. His life was a fable in itself. He was born on a small island, a mere rock, when his mother was fleeing from Norway to the east. Before he reached his uncle in Holmgard (now Novgorod in the U.S.S.R.) he was sold twice as a slave in Estonia; first when he was three years old for a goat, and the second time for a good cloak. His guardian was killed because he was too old to become a slave. Later Olav met the murderer, and the nine-year-old struck him with his axe so that it remained stuck in his skull. As soon as Olav was old enough he went west. He raided and slaughtered whenever he could: Bornholm, Friesland, Germany and England were in his path. He killed people in the Scilly Isles too, but it was there that he was converted to Christianity. After this, he energetically converted Norway, slaying those who were unwilling to receive the Word of Christ. This is how he went about it in Tønsberg, Norway's oldest town:

"King Olav had all these men gathered in a room and had it all well laid out; prepared a great feast for them and gave them strong drink; and when they were drunk Olav had the place set on fire and burnit and all the folk who were therein, except Øyvind Kelde, who got away through the smoke hole." Fortunately he was captured and put on a rock on the west coast, Skratteskjær, where he drowned slowly as the tide rose.

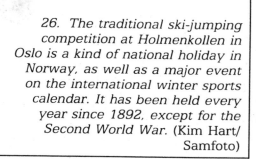

26. The traditional ski-jumping competition at Holmenkollen in Oslo is a kind of national holiday in Norway, as well as a major event on the international winter sports calendar. It has been held every year since 1892, except for the Second World War. (Kim Hart/ Samfoto)

In this manner Norway received the Christian faith.

The other heroic king, Olav Haraldsson (St Olav) used the same method. He let some die and others were mutilated, as the saga tells us. One of life's unsolved mysteries is how he reconciled his missionary activity with the commandment 'Thou shalt not kill'. What is clear is that he was regarded as a saint after his death, and is always called Saint Olav in Norway. The number of statues unveiled in his honour increases, and a play is performed each year in his memory at Stiklestad in Trøndelag, where he was slain in battle. Olsok, 29 July, is commemorated as a special day in his honour.

Before we leave the Vikings it is only fair to mention the good things about them: their excellent laws, their trading activities, their skill in boatbuilding and in fashioning beautiful ornaments, which are still being discovered. Not long ago an extraordinary treasure trove of Viking jewels was literally turned up from under a stone in Grimstad in south Norway.

The country's modern history dates from 1814. Norway was united as one kingdom shortly before the year 900, and flourished in the high Middle Ages — politically, culturally and economically. From 1537 to 1814 Norway was subject to Danish sovereignty, with severe consequences for our language, social organization and history. We gained our independence on 17 May 1814, but only conditionally: we were forced into a union with Sweden and acquired a Swedish king. The nineteenth century was a century of nationalism for Norway.

The rebellious young poetic genuis Henrik Wergeland, who was

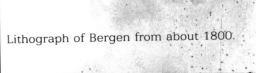

Lithograph of Bergen from about 1800.

described as tall, broad-shouldered, red-cheeked, often on horseback, often drunk, argumentative and fanatical, put all his energy into promoting our independence. He Norwegianized the language, and challenged the king of Sweden by introducing the celebration of 17 May.

P. Chr. Asbjørnsen and Jørgen Moe, following the example of the Brothers Grimm in Germany, collected Norwegian folk tales, and the grammarian Ivar Aasen formed the New Norwegian written language based on Norwegian dialects, an antidote to the dominant Danish language. Artists such as J. C. Dahl, Adolph Tidemand and Hans Gude painted in what has been termed the 'national Romantic' style.

In the political field the left-wing party of the day — *Venstre* — was organized to fight for Norwegian independence and for an extension of suffrage, at that time restricted to professional and wealthy people. The parliamentary system was introduced in 1884; one man one vote in 1898; one woman one vote in 1913. By then the struggle for independence had borne fruit. On the 7 June 1905 Norway became independent of Sweden and chose her own king, the Danish Prince Carl, who took the name Haakon VII.

In this century Norwegian political life has to a great degree been dominated by the struggle for a just distribution of social benefits. The influence of the Left gave way to that of the Labour Party, *Arbeiderpartiet*, which after leaving a somewhat revolutionary past behind it, at least on paper, took office in 1935 in a more or less forced coalition with the Agrarian Party, *Bondepartiet*.

Norway kept out of the First World War, but was occupied by the Germans in the Second. A startled Norwegian people had to stand by and watch an unprepared country being invaded by a force of 10,000 Germans, increasing to 400,000 in the next five years, blasting their way into rocks and cliffs and turning the whole of Norway into a fortress — *Festung Norwegen*.

The small Nazi party (*Nasjonal Samling*) had never had any real influence, yet on the evening of 9 April 1940, the people of Norway heard on their radio an oddly awkward and feeble voice attempting to sound masterful and resolute announcing that the Norwegian Nazi Party had taken over the government of Norway. With this act of usurpation the speaker gave a new name to the concept of treason in all languages: quisling.

Vidkun Quisling, clergyman's son and politician, is still something of a mystery to the Norwegian people. He was undoubtedly of brilliant intelligence, but a fanatic and a dreamer. As a young man he had worked for Fridtjof Nansen providing aid to refugees in Russia, and at the beginning of the 30s he had been minister of defence in the Agrarian Party government. In 1933 he founded the Norwegian Nazi Party. His hour of triumph came in 1940, though he had to play second fiddle all through the war to Hitler's *Reichskommisar für die besetzen Norwegischen Gebiete*, Joseph Terboven, banker and *gauleiter*, who had had the honour of having Hitler as best man at his wedding. Quisling was installed as 'Minister President', though he preferred the German-style *Fører*, and expended great energy in ineffectual efforts to coerce the Norwegian people into embracing Nazism. The king and the country's lawful government went into exile, and took up their position against the Germans from London. At home a clandestine military resistance army, the Home Front, was gradually built up, while the man in the street had his own ways of showing resistance to the occupier. Haakon VII's insignia, a red woollen cap *(nisselua),* and a paper-clip on the lapel were small pinpricks against the occupying forces, yet they found their mark: "From my experience of working in a bank I know that one uses paper clips to fasten documents that one wishes to lay aside. The act of wearing paper clips seems to me to be one of cutting truth: the ex-king and his exile government are in truth stapled together and laid aside!" These were the words of *Reichskommisar* Terboven in his 1 May speech in 1941.

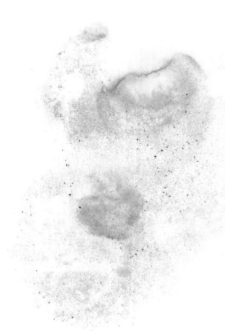

Radios were confiscated, the press was 'Nazified', and stringent food rationing introduced. Some 1,700 Norwegians were killed and wounded in the fighting of 1940. Altogether 10,000 men and women lost their lives at home or abroad in the Second World War. In addition 27,000 Russians died in Norway, either during the liberation of the north of Norway in 1944, or as prisoners of war in German camps. In 1942, 5,000 Yugoslavs were deported by the German Nazis to Norway; only 1,700 survived.

There are more than 20 Yugoslav war cemeteries in Norway, of which the largest is in Botn in Nordland, where 1,657 are buried.

Around 40,000 Norwegians were imprisoned during the war, 19,000 of them in Grini, the prison camp near Oslo, while 8,000 were deported to Germany and German-occupied countries. Among these were Trygve Bratteli and Einar Gerhardsen, later to become prime ministers. Half the prisoners died in captivity. Very few Norwegian Jews survived the war. Altogether 366 Norwegians were executed in Norway and Germany.

Many towns and villages were burnt to the ground, and the entire counties of North Troms and Finnmark were devastated as part of the Germans' scorched-earth policy. The inhabitants were forcibly evacuated south, but 23,000 defied the order and stayed behind, many hiding in caves.

The post-war trials were conducted in a calm manner, and the severity of the punishments diminished with time. The Nazi Party had 55,000 members, 46,000 of whom were later punished for treason. Twelve German and 25 Norwegian Nazis were executed. One of these was Quisling. The German *Reichskommisar* Joseph Terboven committed suicide at Skaugum, the residence of the Norwegian crown prince that he had occupied. Capital punishment has since been abolished in Norway.

Around 9,000 children were born of German fathers in Norway during the war. It was not until the 1980s that they dared to come out publicly and organize themselves. Their mothers had their heads shaved in the chaotic outbreak of peace in May 1945.

Present-day Norway is still characterized by a social democratic way of thinking which has its roots in the lean 30s and also in the spirit of co-operation that went into rebuilding Norway after the war. The former road worker Prime Minister Einar Gerhardsen went straight to the hearts of the Norwegian people with his sober life-style and speech of the common man. Ola Nordmann was proud when he read in the paper that the prime minister and his wife had been spotted on their summer holiday in Italy — in a small tent on a camp-site.

From 1935 until 1963 Norway had a succession of Labour governments, interrupted only by the war. Since 1963 the Labour Party has alternated in office with the Conservatives (in coalition). However, the Conservatives have moved closer to Labour, and Labour closer to the right, so that it is becoming difficult to distinguish between the two major parties. The great period of egalitarianism has made its impact. People no longer address each other by the formal *De*, but use the familiar *du*. The title *Herr* seems to be used by Norwegians as a term of polite abuse.

Some feel the authorities have too much say in regulating the smallest detail of people's lives, but that seems to be an inherited failing among Norwegians. The central authorities have delegated much decision-making, and the country is divided into 18 counties and 454 boroughs, Oslo being both county and borough. The Storting (Parliament) has 165 members, and usually works in plenary sessions, but for certain legislative matters is divided into two chambers, the larger Odelsting and the smaller Lagting.

Each Friday the king meets with the cabinet, which means that ministers make their decisions in the presence of the king. He himself has no political power, but plays an important role as a unifying symbol.

Unlike her neighbours, Norway has never had a large aristocracy, and since 1821 the nobility has been abolished. The first aristocracy was established in the Middle Ages, but died out partly because of the Black Death, partly because a large number became yeoman farmers. A new aristocracy arose in the seventeenth century, many of whose members were descended from Fru Inger of Østraat in Trøndelag, the lady about whom Ibsen wrote a play. A few were elevated to the peerage through their property: Count Ulrik Frederik Gyldenløve of Laurvigen (Larvik), Count Peder Griffenfeldt of Tunsberg (later Jarlsberg), and Baron Ludvig Rosenkrantz of Rosendal in Sunnhordaland, south of Bergen. The family seats at Larvik and Rosendal are now museums, while the manor at Jarlsberg is lived in and run by the eleventh generation of the family in direct line from the first owner. There are still some great landowners, one of them being Harald Løvenskiold' who owns an extensive part of the enormous forest area around Oslo, Nordmarka.

In recent years a new 'aristocracy' has emerged, veritable dynasties of politicians, not least from within the Labour Party. There is also an accumulation of power in the Trades Union Congress (LO — *Landsorganisasjonen*), which has 35 unions and around 870,000 members. Its counterparts, the employers in industry and crafts, have recently amalgamated their organizations into the NHO *(Næringslivets Hovedorganisasjon)*, comprising 1,500 companies and 425,000 employees. However, wage settlements are often left to the politicians.

The international student revolt of 1968 had a strong impact on Norway, less perhaps because of the importance of its main instigator, the small Maoist Communist Party, AKP-ml, than because of the over-reaction of the Conservative press! Whatever the cause, Norway experienced an upsurge of radicalization in the 1970s and early 80s, a spate of labour disputes and demonstrations. Women, pro-abortionists, gays and environmentalists hurled themselves into the fray, battling for their rights, while blue- and white-collar workers, even the clergy, put forward pay claims. There was also the biggest farmers' demonstration ever.

The law declaring homosexuality illegal was repealed in 1972. In 1981 Norway became the first country in the world to pass a law banning discrimination on the grounds of religion, race or sexual proclivity. Gays have their own organization, the Norwegian Federation of 1948. Yet it is one thing to clamp down on overt discrimination, less easy to root out covert discrimination. There was great consternation in the 1980s when a prominent Conservative female politician came out openly as the lover of the woman who was Secretary General of the Norwegian Federation of 1948. She was not re-elected to Parliament. As in other countries, gays are deeply involved in the AIDS debate. By September 1990, 176 cases of AIDS had been registered in Norway; 122 of these have died.

If we are to sum up the main events of post-war Norway, we are left with four dates. In 1949 Norway became a member of NATO after plans failed for a Scandinavian defence union. No passports are required when travelling between the Nordic countries, there is a common labour market, mutual social security schemes, and a considerable reduction of tariffs between the countries. But that is the full extent of the co-operation. On the whole developments have been slow. By 1987 they had, for instance, not been able to come to an agreement on a common Nordic TV-satellite.

The second event, in 1967, attracted less attention, but was of great importance for the individual. A national pensions scheme was introduced, the greatest single social reform in our history. Its aim was to give Norwegians security from cradle to grave, and 20 years later it was to provide the main means of subsistence for one quarter of the population.

On 23 December 1969, the first workable oil well was discovered in the North Sea, and Ola Nordmann turned into an oil sheik.

Lastly, on 22 September 1972, a referendum decided against Norway becoming a member of the European Economic Community. This issue split the nation into two camps, forcing every level of argument into the field and causing enmity between brother and brother, father and son. It is understandable that until the end of the 80s, the Norwegians avoided any further discussion of the matter. But at the beginning of the 90s, the European connection is again the hottest political question. And maybe the mood has changed, so that Norway in a few years may seek EC membership.

It may fairly be said of the post-war period that things have moved in an evolutionary rather than a revolutionary way. Having completed reconstruction work, Norway developed a mania for centralization. Any opportunity to amalgamate was seized; farms, schools, boroughs, banks, dairies, private companies and public institutions were formed into larger units. Thousands of small children had to be picked up by bus rather than walk to the nearest village school. Thousands of workers had to commute long distances to get to work. The country has altogether changed course from one that was socialist-inspired to one that is more purely capitalist and profit-oriented.

There has been liberalization within the domains of the media, licensing laws and the health service. One of the most hotly debated issues of the past decade has been privatization of the public health service. Norway must surely be said to have one of the world's best health services, aiming to treat everyone alike, regardless of status. Any complaints put forward about our health service would seem absurd to someone in Cochabamba or Calcutta. Yet while hospital queues are growing and some hospitals have so little money that they refuse to take in new patients, no politician dares to raise the level of taxation to solve the welfare crisis.

Norway's Social Democrats still call their party the Labour Party, unlike their fellows in Sweden and Denmark. The trouble is that real labourers are not so thick on the ground: they have all turned into consultants, shop assistants and computer salesmen.

The benefits have been reaped, the welfare state is more or less a reality, and the country finds itself at a crossroads.

THE LAND

CHAPTER THREE tells of the amazing variety of our beautiful countryside and how people from Sunnmøre put their money in the bank, while those living in the north invest theirs in Danish pastries.

We don't want to sound boastful, but we must say that the Norwegian landscape is unique. It is so wild, so unspoilt (well, up to a point...) and so varied! There is continuous change, from the wide farmlands of Trøndelag, and east Norway with its large well-kept farms surrounded by dark threatening forests, to the sheltered idyllic Sørlandet; from the wind-blown shores of Jæren, via the towering mountains and plummeting fjords of the west to the weatherbeaten coast of the north with small fishing villages clinging to the rock face; while as a last outpost to the east lie the mighty wastes of Finnmark, wrapped in the dark of total night — or lit by the midnight sun.

As varied as the landscape is the population, even though the last decades have seen a sad tendency towards centralization. "Rural Norway is in the process of turning into a lanky thinly-populated town, while Oslo is a big city whose face is spotty with puberty," declared the Grand Old Man of Norwegian poetry, Rolf Jacobsen, on his eightieth birthday in 1987.

South Norway is divided lengthwise by Langfjellene (literally the Long Mountains), and crosswise by Dovrefjell. These Norwegian mountains are extremely hard. Indeed Dovre is the very symbol of the Norwegian bedrock. 'Faithful, and of one accord, until Dovre fall' was the motto of our political forebears who gathered in 1814 to found the Constitution.

East Norway is a country of long, sloping valleys, large parishes, and forests that stretch deep into Sweden. Here, as elsewhere, primary industries have given way to service industries, tourism and commercial enterprise. Yet this in the land of the big farmers, and the part of the country with the most marked class differences.

Small towns are dotted along the coast of the Oslo fjord, for the south (Sørlandet) is especially the holiday paradise of Norway, with its unique archipelago, skerries and creeks. This is traditionally an outgoing part of the world; that is, the men go to sea, while the women stay home and look after the house. And yet the south and the west have the reputation of being the most puritanical areas, with their chapels,

27. *Svolvær, the biggest fishing port in the Lofoten archipelago, is also a centre of tourism in northern Norway.* (Helge Sunde/ Samfoto)

temperance movements and religious dissenters. This may of course be changing, but the myth remains, and when the state television wants someone to put forward ultra-conservative views, they inevitably find someone from the south.

More stones must have been picked up from the Jæren plain than anywhere else in Norway, and the farmer from Jæren is reckoned to be the country's most painstaking. Today he also makes money from oil, as Rogaland and particularly Stavanger is the main base for the Norwegian oil industry.

The landscape up the west coast must be the most beautiful we have, with long stretches of fjord feeling their way inland under perpendicular rock faces where small farms have maintained a precarious foothold through the ages. You can still see these dwellings in Geirangerfjorden, where all the cruise ships pass. Today most of them are deserted. The French officer Jacques de la Tocnaye tells us in his journal of 1799, *Promenade en Norvège,* what it was like to live in the west:

"On small shelves 700 to 800 feet in the air we see farms which are only accessible if you first climb vertically up a 30- to 40-foot ladder and then clamber up the rocks. The ladder descends straight into the sea, and is firmly attached, so that you can moor your boat to it. With some amazement one notes animals grazing on these shelves, even cows that can only have been conveyed up there as sucking calves on the back of their owner. Bishop Pontoppidan must be right when he relates how a coffin has to be lowered by rope for a burial."

Roads that can be used even in winter have been built across the mountains from east to west, shielded by snow screens and with numerous tunnels. Yet every winter the radio makes announcements about blocked roads and snowed-in cars. Even the Bergen train gets stuck on the Finse plateau between Oslo and Bergen.

The roads have been straightened wherever possible. But take your car up the Trollstigen road in Romsdal or down the old zig-zag route in Måbødalen in Hardanger, and you will get some idea of what it was like to be a driver in Norway in the infancy of the motorcar. It was in these parts that drivers from flat Denmark looked around for locals to take their place at the wheel!

It may be true that Norway is in the process of becoming one continuous town, as our great poet expressed it, and Oslo is certainly in its puberty: '. . . that strange city no one escapes from until it has left its mark on him . . .' as Knut Hamsun wrote in his first novel *Hunger* in the days when the town was still called Christiania. While Copenhagen with its 100,000 citizens in 1800 and Stockholm with 75,000 were reckoned among the great cities of the Continent, Oslo with its population of 12,000 was still a hamlet, a Lilliput on the outskirts of Europe. Today the city has 450,000 citizens and, though still provincial, it has gained an international touch here and there. Immigrants from the Third World run small corner stores — the ones Norwegians closed as unprofitable, and the main street, Karl Johan, is now changed beyond recognition with seething life, musicians and street vendors. As the capital city, Oslo is the seat of the most important institutions: Parliament, government offices, the lawcourts and the royal palace.

In recent times, the capital has been trying to emulate Manhattan by constructing oversized modern buildings in central commercial areas, like Aker Brygge and Grønland/Vaterland. But still it has charm. In the core of the city lies the quadrangular grid of streets founded by the

28. *The island of Landegode, rising 803 metres (2,625 feet) from the sea, shelters the busy town of Bodø, where the railway line to northern Norway ends.* (Husmo-Foto) ▷

29. Varden, high above Molde, offers a magnificent view of the town, and the 87 mountain peaks that form the Romsdal Alps on the other side of the fjord. (Husmo-Foto)

30. Stavanger, Norway's oil capital, has old waterfront houses that conceal restaurants and modern boutiques behind their quaint façades. (Husmo-Foto) ▷

31. The Nidaros Cathedral in Trondheim, built between 1100 and 1300, was an important site of pilgrimage in medieval Europe. (Husmo-Foto) ▷ ▷

36. In the narrow streets of
Stavanger's old town, pedestrians can
stroll unimpeded by cars. Shop signs
reveal that the old trade in herring is
still continued. (Husmo-Foto)

37. In the Middle Ages, Bergen Wharf
was the centre of trade and contacts
with foreign countries. Eleven of the
old buildings remain, having being
restored and preserved. (Helge Sunde)

38

38. The old white wooden houses are to be seen in many towns along the coast, as here in Stavanger. (Husmo-Foto)

39. Bergen has a relatively mild and very rainy coastal climate. The umbrella is not an obligatory part of the daily gear, but a true citizen of Bergen will always have one close at hand. (Helge Sunde)

40. *The attractive old white houses still survive at Mandal on the south coast. One of its streets is named after sculptor Gustav Vigeland, who was born here.* (R. Lislerud/Samfoto)

40

41. *A pale winter sun shines over the harbour of Oslo and the castle of Akershus, which gives the city its seaside profile.* (Kim Hart/Samfoto)

42. In November the sun can still be
seen on the mountains around
Hammerfest, before winter darkness
descends on this town, the most
northerly in the world. (O. Åsheim/
Samfoto)

43. Ålesund on the west coast is
above all a fishing community. After
a big fire in 1904, the centre was
rebuilt in Art Noveau style. (T. Bølstad/
Samfoto)

44. Norway's southern coast usually
has quite mild winters, but sometimes
a spell of cold weather may cause
trouble for seagoing traffic, as here in
the harbour of Risør. (M. Løberg/
Samfoto)

45

45. The old city bridge with its distinctive 'portals' connects the two halves of Trondheim, on either side of the river Nidelva. (Husmo-Foto)

46. Arendal is a busy seaside town and a centre for cruising and holidaying on the sunny south coast of Norway. (Mittet)

47. The Nidaros Cathedral in Trondheim, the largest medieval building in Scandinavia. Before the Reformation in 1536, it was the seat of an archbishop. (Husmo-Foto) ▷

48. Molde is known as the city of roses, and the 'Rose Girl', by sculptress Ragnhild Butenschøn, has her basket filled with golden roses in summertime. Large parts of the town were destroyed during the war (in 1940), so that Molde today has much modern architecture, like the church in the background. (Husmo-Foto) ▷ ▷

49. Along the sounds and inlets under the jagged peaks of the Lofoten mountains nestle small fishing communities with characteristic old houses. (R. Frislid/NN) ▷ ▷ ▷

Danish-Norwegian Renaissance monarch Christian IV, whose name the city bore for so long. Since those days Oslo has steadily expanded, eating up the surrounding fields in the last century, and now extending its suburbs well into neighbouring boroughs. You get out there by underground and local trains, but don't lose heart if no one talks to you! Not that Oslo dwellers are slow and taciturn. It's just that they bear in them a dream of forests and lonely mountain spaces that they try to relive as often as they can.

And they do have the opportunity, for the city is surrounded by extensive and wonderful woodland, in fact one of the largest areas of forest in Norway. People use this forestland, Nordmarka or Marka, both summer and winter. On a fine day there can be over 100,000 people in Nordmarka; in winter they take the train to the northern edge of the forest and ski the 40 to 50 kilometres (25 to 30 miles) home. Nordmarka is sacred to Oslo-dwellers with its thousands of snow crystals glittering against the winter light, its birdsong fading in the pale summer nights, the blue anemones of spring, or when Nature puts on her glowing autumn garments. When hydroelectric developers wanted to lay their hands on Marka in 1946, 40,000 people protested in front of the City Hall — and they won!

But is it not rainy Bergen that is Norway's number one city — at least according to people from Bergen? "I'm not from Norway; I'm from Bergen" they sing in their characteristic dialect. So what is Bergen? It is Bryggen, the Wharf — its earlier name, German Wharf, was dropped in 1945 after the occupation, though it dates from the Hanseatic time. With its wooden buildings in a style unchanged since the Middle Ages, it is a collection of intriguing small houses that creep up the hillsides. It is a city of extraordinary military bands of small boys (*Buekorpsene*) that march out with wooden guns and awake the town with drumbeats every Sunday morning. Bergen is the city under the seven hills, with the waters of Puddefjorden and Vågen stretching right up to the fish market. For it was fish that made the town, dried fish from the north that was shipped on from Bergen. Bergen was one of the most important Hanseatic towns, a relic of which is the large number of foreign names.

Trondheim, too, has an aura of history. An ancient site of pilgrimage, it was the seat of an archbishopric that covered Norway, the Hebrides and the Isle of Man, the Orkney and Shetland Islands, Iceland and Greenland. Scandinavia's most magnificent cathedral, Nidarosdomen, is a monument to this. High in the air like a pinnacled saint stands Olav Tryggvason, founder of the town and brutal missionary. His later descendant, Olav Haraldson, did actually become a saint, and is the reason for all the pilgrimages. Like Bergen, Trondheim is a university town, especially proud of its technological university. Trondheim and Bergen compete for the position of second most important city of Norway.

And now to north Norway. To any one from the south this seems an infinite distance away. Just take a look at the map. When you get to Bodø, you're only half-way up. You have to lay four maps of Denmark in a row to get from Trondheim in mid-Norway to Kirkenes furthest north-east.

Most 'southerners' know little about north Norway. They may have been to the Canaries or Majorca, but it's unlikely they will have visited Neiden or Brøstadbotn. Which is a pity, for the north has scenery as wild and as unexpected as that of the west. One of the greatest experiences is

50. A granite lion guards the building of the Storting, Norway's national assembly. (Husmo-Foto)

to travel by the coastal express (*Hurtigruta*) and see the cliff face of Lofoten rising sheer above Vestfjorden. It is by following the coastline that you can see how Norway was made. The coast will give you proof of the Norwegians' amazing ability to find a foothold in the smallest cracks. Wherever there is a few spare feet of beachline under a rock face, you can be sure someone has staked his claim to it and planted his state-mortgaged house. There, with his fishing-smack, he abandons himself to the sea and his own devices, the fog-horn and the lighthouse beam.

Along the whole coastline there are lighthouses guiding ships to safety. Yet the lighthouse keeper is a disappearing breed, and now only 65 out of Norway's 200 lighthouses are manned. When the rationalization programme is completed, there will be even fewer. Even the horn, background music to seafaring people on foggy nights, is threatened in our age of advanced technology.

There are 33 lifeboats ready to go out to ships in distress. These have been paid for with money raised through sales and raffles by a thousand organizations working voluntarily for the Life Boat Society throughout Norway.

The north Norwegian journalist, Arthur Arntzen, said something very beautiful about life on the north Norwegian coast when interviewed by the Oslo paper *Aftenposten:*

"As a journalist I have on a couple of occasions found myself present in a fishing village when boats with five or six men have gone down. But grief takes a strange shape in these outlying places. It is not hysterical. There is a calmness in grief in places like this. I noticed there were no tears over losing a son or a father. As if they accepted that his days were over — that what had been had been good. This uprightness and firmness is perhaps learnt from living close to the sea and the mighty forces of nature. So unlike town..."

He also said something about another side of the northerner, his amazingly inventive language, something the writer Knut Hamsun took south. If you take the oaths away from a northerner, you take half his language, Arntzen said.

The north is not without cities. There is Hammerfest, the northern-most town in the world. And there is Tromsø, the 'Paris of the North', the liveliest town in Norway, with its marvellous people, its university, its famous Mack beer, and its Arctic cathedral. There is, of course, the tundra where reindeer feed, and where the Såmi pitch camp, but you also find more gentle wooded landscapes in this wild territory, in the Pasvik Valley on the Russian border, or in Målselv or Bardufoss in Troms. Then you have extraordinary natural phenomena such as the Torghatten mountain with a hole in it, and the Moskenes whirlpool, the mælstrom described by both Edgar Allan Poe and Jules Verne.

There is also Nordkapp, the most northerly plateau in the world, visited yearly by some 100,000 tourists who want to see the midnight sun. Weather permitting! On 1 July 1987, there was a snowstorm on Nordkapp. Unfortunately the Norwegian sense of inferiority has man-ifested itself here too. With the south already overrun by holiday parks with dinosaurs, Gullivers and Donald Duck shows, it seems that the Scandinavian mega-corporations, SAS and Kosmos, decided that Nord-kapp wasn't selling properly. They therefore blasted out some hundred tons of rock to make way for restaurants and other facilities. One of these is a huge screen, curved 200 degrees, where Nordkapp can be artificially experienced in 3D and stereo sound. There is also a grotto and a tunnel that leads to a 10-metre-wide (33-foot) panoramic window of the sea. From Nordkapp the tourists can link up directly with America's number one amusement park in Florida – via a Walt Disney satellite. ''They have ruined everything,'' said a German tourist, who wept when he saw what was being done to Nordkapp in 1987. In 1990 an extensive area of the plateau was turned into a parking lot, where hundreds of his compatriots, video-cameras made ready, sleep in their campers, waiting for the midnight sun. But the northerner lets these things happen, even when the authorities ask him to stay away from the North Cape so as not to disturb the tourists!

''The northerner is Norway's dreamer and fantast, the one who cuts a dash. I wonder whether he is not in many ways the incarnation of the soul of Norway? When a *Sunnmøring* comes home after a trip to the fishing grounds, he has earned 400 kroner. He puts 400 kroner in the bank. When a northener comes home from a fishing trip, he has earned 200 kroner. He spends 20 on a silk scarf for his sweetheart, and the rest on Danish pastries! His personal motto is: 'One must have a little enjoyment in life'.''

This is taken from the 1965 novel *Rubicon* by one of Norway's most translated post-war novelists, Agnar Mykle. Coming from a Sunnmøre family from the west and having lived in the north, he ought to know what he is talking about.

People from Sunnmøre are said to be the most industrious in

Medieval stave church, Borgund, western Norway.

Norway. Who else would dream of starting a furniture industry in a part of the world where hardly a tree grows? Meanwhile the northerners keep up the myth of the pastries. North Norway has always been dependent on the south. In olden days the fishermen of the north had to sell their catch in Bergen. The Frenchman Jacques de la Tocnaye described the results of this a couple of centuries ago:

"The tradesmen are skilful at tempting them, and never let them go home without a hefty debt, and as they buy everything on credit, this can mount up to 20,000 rix-dollars (a silver coin worth 4 kroner). As security they stake their farms with live and dead stock, thus putting themselves entirely in the power of the tradespeople. These take care to renew the loans, so that the fishermen never become free."

It is the people from Sunnmøre who make the profit from the fish in the north — at least according to the fishermen from the north. Our present fisheries policy is formed in the east to benefit the west. Western Norway has built up a large sea-going fishing fleet, while the man from Finnmark sticks close to the shore with his hand-held line and lead sinker. Finnmark has once more become a crofting community compared with the rich west country, they say.

Not only that. North Norway is becoming depopulated. The drop of 10,000 in the region's population in the last five years alone is the largest since the nineteenth century. In Finnmark there are 1,000 fewer people each year. This hurts in a county with only 75,000 inhabitants.

It is essential to keep up the population of the north because of the fish and the possible oil resources in the Barents Sea. Much political debate in recent years has been concerned with how to stop the population drifting away. Newpapers in the south are continually referring to the lack of skilled persons in the north. We hear about all the vacant teaching jobs in secondary schools, about police constables being posted north to Vardø, and about the only doctor in Berlevåg 'escaping' from the strain.

It is indeed quite a transition for someone from, say, Toten, to become parish priest in Loppa, an island right out in the Arctic Ocean. Toten is reputed to be the most introspective and inbred place in Norway. 'Damn Norway — long live Toten' is the stock saying. On Loppa Bård Jahr Pettersen has to cater for the spiritual welfare of a parish that is spread over 11 hamlets, many of them accessible only by boat. There are seven churches in the parish and he has to conduct 112 church services, 20 funerals, up to 10 weddings and the confirmation of 50 young souls. One church service can take as long as 11 hours with the journey there and back.

Many suggestions have been made for political solutions to the north Norway question, and a number of 'Finnmark Deals' have been launched to provide decent conditions for the population. Some say taxation should be removed, others say that more should be spent on aid for regional development. Some occupational groups already receive state support — health workers, teachers and administrators — but not the girls who slice fillets of cod in icy rooms. And what Finnmark really needs is girls — girls and people with education. Many feel that the main priority should be education and research. There is a tendency for people who study in the region to stay there.

The tradition of the south providing aid to the north is a venerable one. Under a bequest made in 1621 by a clergyman's wife, Ingeborg Mikkeldatter, 500 kilos (1,100 pounds) of flour were to be handed out to the poor and needy of Øksnes every Christmas in perpetuity, bought with the interest on the 300 old Norwegian dollars she left as a legacy. These 500 kilos of flour are still being sent to Nordland from Vaksdal Mills in Bergen!

The local government minister in 1987, William Engseth, is from the north himself, but told the northerners to stop moaning and groaning. He says that the north is a land of opportunity, but its people must have the sense to make use of their resources, investing in fishing, fish farms, minerals and tourism. The air is clean and there is plenty of hunting and fishing. He does not think that the plans for the north should be drawn up by people sitting in Oslo, but that they should be made on the northerners' own terms. And he thinks it is nonsense to believe anyone will establish themselves on a rock in the north for 50 weeks a year in order to lie on a Mediterranean beach for two weeks. He was here referring to the Soviet practice of using free holidays in the south to tempt people to move to the Kola Peninsula, where they also receive higher wages and better housing than their compatriots in more central regions. The result is that the population in the north of the Soviet Union has increased. Today there are almost a million people living on the Kola Peninsula, 450,000 of them in Murmansk, the large Arctic city near the border with Finnmark.

Today many people in Finnmark want to build a 40-kilometre (25-mile) railway line from Kirkenes to the Soviet industrial city Nikel, which is connected by rail to the rest of the Soviet Union. Nikel (population 300,000) is easily visible from the hills in the Pasvik Valley. There is already lorry traffic between the two towns. Kirkenes intends to invest heavily in increased trade with the U.S.S.R.

The town also wants to take on ship repairs for the Russians. The linchpin of industry in Kirkenes is the state-owned mining company A/S Sydvaranger, now in danger of being closed down, as it is proving too costly to extract the necessary iron ore. A/S Sydvaranger has therefore partly amalgamated with the giant Finnish shipyard Wärtilä and started KIMEK, the engineering works at Kirkenes, which aims at having the Soviet fleet as its main customer. The Russians certainly have enough ships to repair if you count all their fishing vessels, ice-breakers and floating oil installations.

This is Norway, from east to west, north to south, wilderness and waste, oil kingdom and city. You can reach it all, by car and boat, by train

Medieval farm drawn by Ken Ole Moen after excavations in Handøy, northern Norway.

or plane. There are 4,200 kilometres (2,600 miles) of railway from Oslo to Stavanger, Bergen and Bodø. The Nordland railway is planned to reach Harstad, but is unlikely ever to get there. The country has 85,000 kilometres (53,000 miles) of public road — 50 times the length of the country stretched out. This road network includes 225 car ferries. Norway is the land of the car ferry: many memories of summer holidays include long waits in narrow fjords, with refreshments from the ice-cream shop and children on the quay selling baskets of freshly picked strawberries and cherries. Some 50 million passengers a year travel by boat in Norway, and 45 million of them are car ferry passengers. The others take small boats to outlying islands and into fjords where there are no roads.

Annually, 275,000 passengers sail on the *Hurtigruta*, the coastal express. This is an adventure in itself! 'The world's most beautiful coastal route' takes you from Bergen to Kirkenes through narrow straits and over the open sea, past rocky islands and cliffs, stopping at 36 ports of call, summer and winter. Before air travel this was the only year-round southbound route. Today airways have brought the northern region closer to the capital and to the Continent — if you can afford to fly. Less than five per cent of the total Norwegian passenger transport in 1984 was airborne.

If the Norwegian mainland has not satisfied your need for wild countryside, there are still the islands to the north, although it is hardly desirable to expand tourist activity in those areas. 'Svalbard discovered' was reported by the Icelanders in 1194, and since 1925 Norway has had sovereignty over this island in the Barents Sea.

The Svalbard Treaty, with around 40 nations as signatories, opened the island to development and enterprise from nations other than Norway. Today Russians and Norwegians both have coalmines on Svalbard, living there without much communication. The Norwegians' main base is Longyearbyen, where the midnight sun shines from April, and where there is a school and a hospital, a flight to Norway two or three times a week, and satellite radio, television and telephone. In 1985 there were 1,386 Norwegians on Svalbard, 2,549 Russians, 11 Poles, and eight of other nationalities. The Russians are based in Barentsburg.

Though not publicized, there is tourism on Svalbard, including ski scooter trips in temperatures as low as minus 35 °C, and the limited accommodation of the Norwegian mining company has up to 70,000 guest nights. People also stay through the winter on the meteorological stations on the other islands besides Svalbard: Jan Mayen, Bjørnøya (Bear Island) and Hopen. Every Christmas the newspapers telephone from the mainland to find out if the Christmas mail has arrived and to get stories about 'overwinterers' who have had to use frying-pans to ward off polar bears trying to break into their huts. There have been 50 serious confrontations between polar bears and humans since the polar bear became a protected species in 1973. Svalbard is the only place in Norway where rabies has been registered, carried by the Arctic fox, reindeer and seals, though not by polar bears. There are at least 10,000 Arctic foxes on the island.

There are those who dream of Svalbard turning into a kind of Arctic centre, with two international airports, a Hilton hotel, oil and gaspipes to the mainland, and a permanent road linking the two island 'metropolises'. This is likely to remain a dream. Unless, of course, someone from Sunnmøre does something about it.

THE SÅMI

CHAPTER FOUR is the story of how the Norwegians conquered Lappland, and how the Såmi miraculously managed to salvage some of their cultural identity.

I confess I am a Såmi, said one of the participants at a conference of Coast Såmi in Finnmark in 1982. Confess! This reveals the full extent of the discrimination against the Såmi; this proves the success of the majority in oppressing them; this shows how long the Norwegians had been telling them they belonged to an inferior race. And yet there was promise in the word. He did confess rather than deny he was a Såmi, as his people had done for so long to avoid discrimination.

The Såmi language still lives! To a Norwegian it is an exciting experience to hear children chattering in Såmi in the streets of the village of Kautokeino. You get the feeling of being among the Quechua Indians in an Andean village, let's say in Appillapampa in Bolivia!

Three tribes meet in the north: the Såmi (Lapps), the Finns and the Norwegians. No-one has yet traced a connection between the Komsa people who lived in Finnmark 10,000 years ago and the population of Finnmark today, yet of the three races, it was most likely the Såmi who came first.

They appear in the writings of the Roman historian Tacitus in the year A.D. 100. The north Norwegian chieftain Ottar of Helgeland related in the ninth century how he collected taxes from the Lapps in the north. Exploitation can be traced back a long way. So can the first of many derogatory descriptions that were to pursue them through the ages:

"Even in the summer there is much snow, and just as they do not differ much from wild beasts in judgement, nor do they eat anything but the raw flesh of wild animals. They make their clothing of skins." This was written by the Lombard historian Paul around the year 800.

They were an independent people, living in their own country, Såmiid Ædnan, and they knew no boundaries. Within their own territory they had their own little communities, or *siida*, consisting of 40 to 300 people. There were enormous common lands for hunting and fishing open to all. They lived under skies that compelled a mystic worship of nature, with the glowing sun pursuing them from around the horizon all summer, but disappearing in winter and leaving them in darkness on the endless tundra, alone with the silence, the wolf howls and the fantastic, ever-changing northern lights, the cold and biting snowstorms, and the sea that beats more fiercely against the east coast of Finnmark than most

51. The U-shaped valleys and fjords were carved out by ice, and glaciers still hang above the narrow valleys. This is the famous Briksdalsbreen at Olden in Njordfjord. (Husmo-Foto)

other places in the world. Even the coastal express sometimes has to seek harbour.

This was the life of the Lapps, hunters and fishermen, at one with nature, at peace with their gods. The rivers and fjords were teeming with fish, cloudberries grew on the ground, and the reindeer grazed on the tundra, finding their own summer and winter pastures — they were not yet tamed.

No-one knows the origin of the Lapps or Såmi. In their own mythical tradition, as told by the Såmi author Ailo Gaup, the Sun's daughter was the mother of the sons of the sons of the Sun, the heroes of legend. From the sons of the Sun descended the shaman of the *siida*, the *noiade*, priest and medicine man of the village, wise man and healer, conjuring up spirits with his supernatural powers. He officiated at the animal sacrifices that were made outdoors in front of a sacred stone, the *sieidia*, or a carved wooden deity. Able to speak to the spirits, he could get in touch with ancestors and bring feritility, good reindeer pasture, good hunting and plentiful fish. The *noiade* of the Såmi was akin to the Tadiber of the Samoyeds, the Angakod of the Inouits, and the medicine man of the North American Indian tribes. The Såmi had many gods: for birth and well-being, for the heavens, and for the air. The *noiade* had two aids when worshipping: the monotone chant — the *joik* — and the runic drum — *runebommen*.

The *joik* was originally a religious song and formed part of the identity of the Såmi, each person having his own separate *joik*. The runic drum could be as large as three metres (10 feet) across and was inscribed with the entire cosmology of the Såmi: the gods in their universe, the humans in theirs, the sun, the moon, the stars, and the tundra. When the *noiade* beat the drum he used a piece of reindeer antler and some antler figures, which he laid on top of the drumskin. His prophecies were based on the way the antler figures performed during the drumming. To get properly into contact with the spirits, he had to work himself up into a state of ecstasy. The name of the solar deity was Bæivve, and the symbol of the sun was in the centre of the runic drum. Fire sacrifices were also made to the sun. There were many manifestations of solar worship, something that is perfectly comprehensible to anyone who has experienced the Finnmark tundra by midnight sun.

Right up to recent times there has been a strong fear of the Såmi's magic powers, of his sorcerer's arts, his ability to cast a spell over 'both Weather and Water', as the poet and clergyman Peter Dass wrote in his *Nordland Trumpet* in the seventeenth century.

Less than enchanted with the Såmi culture were their neighbours. The Norwegians were only there for the material benefits of the north, the furs and the fish, the feathers, the eider-down, and the game. More and more Norwegians moved north and were joined by Swedes and Finns, Karelians and Russians. They brought with them taxation, trade, colonization and a demand for territory.

Many came carrying a Bible. The Lapp religion was looked upon as idolatry and devil-worship, and Christianity was imposed by law. The death penalty was prescribed for Lapps who would not give up their religion, and their shamans, the *noiades*, could be burnt at the stake for refusing to convert.

In the eighteenth century, the 'Apostle of Finnmark', Thomas von Westen, carried out his inquisition of the Lapps, burning their altars and destroying the runic drums. A missionary in the Lofoten Islands burnt 40

52. New types of sport have reached the Norwegian mountains in winter, for instance, paragliding by means of snow scooters. The picture is from Tyin in the Jotunheim mountain massif. (Husmo-Foto) ▷

53

53. Riding has became a winter sport, and for many people makes a pleasant change from skiing. Many hotels keep a string of Fjording or Iceland ponies, hardy breeds that make headway through the snow. (Husmo-Foto)

54. The horse has enjoyed a renaissance as a riding animal and for the traditional sledge ride, made with burning torches on winter evenings. (Husmo-Foto) ▷

55. *When summer comes, those who miss the snow can cross a glacier on a mountain hike, as in this picture, where the route to Norway's highest peak, Gald høpiggen, (2,469 metres, 8,073 feet) leads across the glacier of Styggebreen. (Hèlge Sunde)* ▷ ▷

56. *Reflected by a shining white wall of snow, the Easter sun is twice as brilliant. (Husmo-Foto)* ▷ ▷ ▷

57

57. Sometimes only the chimney rises above the snow when the owner comes to his mountain cabin for the Easter vacation. But as long as the sun shines and the skiing is good, everyone is happy. (Husmo-Foto)

58. Not everyone is a champion, but it helps to be able to practise on last winter's snow in the July sunshine. The picture is from Strynefjellet in western Norway. (Mittet)

59. In the extensive forests around Oslo there are cabins where skiers can drop in for a cup of coffee. Here all cars are banned – skis are the sole means of travel. (Pål Hermansen/Samfoto)

60. In the cold season, people wrap up warmly and even seem to enjoy getting frosty hair and eyebrows. (Johan Brun/NN)

60

61. Norwegians are not born with their skis on, as the saying goes, but most learn the art of skiing at a very early age. For many, a trip to the mountains or woods is an obligatory exercise on a winter holiday. (F. Friberg NN)

62. Motorized vehicles for use in snowy conditions may be gaining ground, but the horse still makes itself useful in deep snow. (Mittet) ▷

Lapp altars in the course of only two weeks. The priest forbade the *joik*, and demanded that the children be baptized with Norwegian or biblical names, despite the stong tradition of family name among the Sámi. This enforced conversion to Christianity was part of the struggle between the national states over Lappland, as they then called it. The Norwegians had built both a fortress and a church in Vardø in the fourteenth century. By the end of the seventeenth century there were Norwegian churches in all places of any importance in Finnmark. The Russian Orthodox Church came to East Finnmark in the sixteenth century, and there is still a small Orthodox chapel in Neiden. The Swedish Church came later.

The Danish-Norwegian Renaissance king, Christian IV, went right up to the Kola Peninsula in 1599 in order to levy taxes, and at the same time the Russians from Novgorod considered the whole of Finnmark as their taxable property. The Sámi were squeezed by double exploitation, Sámiid Ædnan was drained of resources, and by the seventeenth century Lapp society had disintegrated.

Immigration continued. In the eighteenth century waves of Finns came to Lyngen, Alta and Tana, driven by famine in the forests of Finland. There was fish to attract them to the coast, while the valleys were now opened up to agriculture and grazing. The most intense period of immigration was in the 1860s, when some fishing villages became one hundred per cent Finnish. By then the national states were no longer content with taxing the Sámi; they had also occupied their territory.

In the Middle Ages the northern states had not drawn up any boundaries in the north. Before 1750 the land of the Sámi was described as 'the Lapp nation', or as a 'foreign nation' that did not belong to the kingdom. Then the neighbouring states simply divided up this nation among themselves. Sweden and Norway decided upon their border through Sámi territory in 1751. The nomadic 'Reindeer Sámi' were permitted to move their herds over the new border as before, but the rights of the other tribes to use the land of their forefathers went unrecognized. The border between Norway and Russia was demarcated in 1826. Thus the whole of the country was swallowed up by the conquerors. The Sámi had to adapt to the existence of a minority group, submitting to colonial powers that followed the classic pattern in destroying their ethnic identity.

While the white man in North America used the semblance of a contract to cheat the Indians of their territory, the Norwegians did not even bother to do that. In 1843 the Ministry of Finance established that there was no Crown property in Finnmark; five years later the Ministry proclaimed the whole county the property of the Crown, without any kind of negotiations with the Sámi. "Finnmark proper has from ancient times been considered as belonging to the King or the State, because it was originally only inhabited by a nomad people, the Lapps, who have no permanent habitations,'' the Ministry pronounced, and concluded that "Finnmark has from the most ancient times been considered a colony.''

So the Sámi were driven away by Norwegian settlers.

From 1902 they were not even granted permission to buy their own land if they could not speak Norwegian. This discriminating law was not repealed until 1965. The most urgent task of the colonial power was to get rid of the native language. The Church vacillated in its attitude: some clergymen thought the Sámi should be converted in their own language, while others wanted to eradicate it entirely.

An extraordinary figure in the history of the Sámi is the Swedish

63. The mountains have no shortage of hotels and tourist stations, big and small, all of them packed with happy skiers in the winter and Easter vacations. This picture is from the central valley of Gudbrandsdal in southern Norway. (Husmo-Foto)

botanist and priest Lars Levi Læstadius, who started an exceedingly pietistic revival movement in the last century: the Læstadian movement, as it has been called. He moralized and chastized the Såmi, taking on the role of both father and teacher to the impoverished farmers and nomad Lapps. He hated excess and drunkenness, and especially the liquor that wrought havoc among the Såmi. He called it 'liquid Devil's shite'. But he spoke to the Såmi in their own language and respected them for what they were. For this reason he still has supporters and some congregations follow his teachings, for instance in Alta, Ibostad and Lyngen.

His teachings were to some extent behind the so-called Kautokeino Rising of 1852, when 30 adults and 19 children attacked members of the Swedish-Norwegian upper class. The Læstadian movement demanded total abstinence, and did to a certain degree curb the Såmi's drinking of spirits. This strict religion, with its insistence on penance and contrition, often assumed ecstatic forms. During the services people worked themselves into a state of frenzy, laughing and crying out. It did not help matters when the bishop sent the masterful clergyman Nils Joachim Christian Vibe Stockfleth to sort things out. He was a man who liked his drink and was generous in sharing his brandy keg with the Såmi he met on his visitations.

There were more of his kind. "There were idle and self-satisfied clergymen who lived in ease and luxury with scarcely a thought for their poor parishioners. Some were drawn in reindeer sleds from one wind-blown chapel to the next, often so drunk when they arrived that they had to be tipped out of the sled and lugged into the warmth of the chapel like a carcase of meat." This is how Tor Edvin Dahl described them in Norway's cultural history.

The Rev. Stockfleth personally beat up the 'enthusiasts' in Kautokeino using his pastoral cane. He dismissed the Såmi constable from office and installed a Swede who was held to be a scoundrel. When the parish priest, who was much disliked, went so far as to take lodgings with the hated liquor retailer, the Såmi's religious indignation boiled over and they took action. They horsewhipped the sinful Norwegians and killed both the constable and the publican, though they spared the life of the priest — out of a deep respect for religion.

A trial followed: 33 persons were tried, 27 convicted, and five condemned to death, though three of them were pardoned. Aslak Haatta and Mons Somby were beheaded in Alta on 14 October 1854. One of the 'enthusiasts' had already been beaten to death by guards while the

Lapps hunting on skis. Illustration to Olaus Magnus: 'History of the Nordic Peoples', Rome 1555.

prisoners were being transferred from Kautokeino to the prison in Alta. The central powers sent an infantry unit of 50 men to Alta to restore law and order — an act that was to be repeated over a century later.

The great Norwegianization process started in the 1850s and lasted well into our age. Såmi children were forced to learn Norwegian at school, and their own language was presented as inferior. It was not until 1967 that Norwegian law gave teachers the opportunity to use Såmi as an auxiliary language, and only in 1985 was it legalized as a teaching medium in school. Many who come from Såmi homes speak little Norwegian when they start school. The result of the linguistic coercion has been that only about half the Såmi population is literate. Norwegianization was not confined to the school system. Norwegians assumed power at all levels of society, buildings and properties were given Norwegian names, and the official language was Norwegian even in places that were entirely Såmi.

`The result of this degradation was predictable. At the 1891 census 20 per cent of the population of Troms and Finnmark declared they were Såmi; by 1970 the figure was four per cent.

Yet there is hope for change. On 29 May 1987, a milestone in Såmi history, the Storting passed a new Såmi Law, stating for the first time that there are two population groups in Norway and that the State has a duty to ensure that the Såmi population can preserve its own culture and language. This law was the result of two factors. One was the growing interest in aboriginal peoples and the conditions of minority groups that emerged all over the world in the 1960s. The other was the clash between the promoters of hydroelectric development schemes and environmentalists in 1970 and in the 1980s that culminated in serious unrest in Finnmark. A force of 600 policemen collected from all over the country was sent by troop carrier to remove the conservationists who were out to save the Alta-Kautokeino river; these were Såmi, 'Greens', and intellectuals, who linked themselves together to form great human chains on the building site.

The environmentalists had previously staged demonstrations against hydroelectric schemes in the south, but in Alta their interests coincided with those of the ethnic minority. In the initial plans of 1968 the whole Såmi community of Masi was to have been submerged. Even in the more moderate plans put forward ten years later, many sites that were an important part of the Såmi cultural heritage were threatened, as was some magnificent landscape and valuable pastureland. In the 1970s

Reindeer sledge, 'like a boat or shoe'. Illustration to Olaus Magnus: 'History of the Nordic Peoples', Rome 1555.

there were many demonstrations against the scheme, and Alta became the country's most contentious issue. In Oslo a group of Såmi went on hunger-strike in front of the Parliament buildings, and devout Såmi women squatted in Prime Minister Gro Harlem Brundtland's office, praying and singing hymns, until they were removed by the police.

The conflict that brought strife right into people's families culminated on 14 January 1981, when the 600 policemen from the troop ship *Janina* forcibly removed the 'chain gang'. Altogether 900 people were arrested. Many hundreds were fined. Half those arrested were from the north of Norway, the rest from the south, from Finland and elsewhere. Some of the activists keep the police summons, framed, as a memento.

By 1987 the 115-metre-high (377-foot) dam was finished – ahead of schedule – ready to provide 30,000 families with power. Gro Harlem Brundtland, who was prime minister during the Alta fight, and since has been called the 'world minister of the environment' because of her work as chairman for the United Nations environmental report, caused some consternation in 1990 when she told Norwegian papers that it had not been necessary to build the dam! Until the Såmi Law was passed in 1987, the Såmi were one of the few minority groups in Europe that had no legal recognition. This law establishes that ''the State is bound to ensure that the Såmi population have the material conditions in which to foster their own culture and maintain their language, as well as influence over the physical and economic basis of their culture.'' In practical terms, the law allows for a Såmi parliament – a *ting*. (In neighbouring Finland there has been the equivalent of this since 1973.) This is to deal with Såmi matters, starting by advising government, county and local authorities, and assuming more authority with time. The Såmi parliament – or *Såmeting* – consists of 39 members, chosen from 13 geographical constituencies, based on a population census of the Såmi. Anyone who regards himself as a Såmi can put himself on the electoral roll.

The highly controversial issue of the Såmi's rights to land and water is not touched by the Såmi Law. It is an exceedingly complicated matter. Before the Nordic states occupied their territory, the Såmi had many traditional rights of the kind that nomadic people need in order to survive: rights relating to grazing reindeer and cattle, salmon fishing, catching whales and seals, felling timber, gathering hay and peat from common land, picking cloudberries, collecting eggs and feathers. As these rights have never been sold, the activists assert that the Såmi still own them. The problem is how to reclaim them in a society so totally changed from that of the ancient Såmiid Ædnan. There is no reason to believe that the colonial power will give up its acquisitions without a struggle.

The Såmi are as politically divided as any other people, and their reaction to the new legislation was not unanimous. It is hardly a simple task to create unity in a minority at such an advanced stage of Norwegianization. The superstructure of the Såmi is a Nordic Såmi Conference, held every third year in Sweden, Finland and Norway by turns. The Russian Såmi do not take part. There is nonetheless no real separatist movement, though there are some who claim that the Såmi should have their own independent state.

There are an estimated 50,000 Såmi in the world today: 2,000 on the Kola Peninsula in the Soviet Union, 5,000 in Finland, 15,000 in Sweden, and 30,000 in Norway. The exact figure is difficult to ascertain, as the borders between the different population groups are undefined, and many will not admit to being Såmi. As a young man from Guovdageaidnu (Kautokeino) put it: "I am a Såmi; I own reindeer. But my brother is not a Såmi; he is a car mechanic."

How extensive the land of the Såmi once was remains a matter of academic debate. There are still at least nine different Såmi dialects, found from the Kola Peninsula in the U.S.S.R. to Elga in south Norway. Not all Såmi understand each other's dialect. Also some dialect areas are very small: Lulesåmi is spoken by only 2,000 people from Lulea in Sweden to Hamarøy in Norway, childhood home of Knut Hamsun.

It is a common misconception that only the lasso-throwing, colourfully dressed reindeer-owner is a Såmi. Even in the most exclusively Såmi areas, only 20 per cent of the population is involved in keeping reindeer. Only a couple of thousand Såmi altogether keep reindeer in Norway. Until the Second World War their way of life was more or less the same as when the reindeer was tamed in the seventeenth century. Since the war there have been drastic changes for the Såmi, as for other Norwegians. River boats have been equipped with outboard motors, and Finnmark is the county in Norway with the greatest number of the motorized ski-scooters that have replaced the reindeer sled. Yet it is among the Reindeer Såmi that the Såmi culture has been best preserved. The reindeer follow the same paths, and the knowledge of weather, beasts, and countryside that it takes to move 100,000 reindeer every year is not learnt in five minutes, but over generations. The animals are moved from their winter grazing on the Finnmark tundra to the coast, where the calving takes place and where the animals need to be watched day and night. From there they go to summer pastures and then back again. These huge migrations occasionally lead to conflict with the locals, as in 1987 when the population of Nordkyn tried to deter thousands of reindeer from crossing over Hopsland to their summer pastures. They were impeding road construction works...

It is the reindeer herdsman who has kept his beautiful jacket *(kofte)* as an everyday garment. The Såmi from Hattfjelldal and Snåsa in the south, who also keep reindeer, wear theirs for festive occasions only. Except in Nesseby and Tysfjord, the Coast Såmi have let theirs go out of use, and when they wanted to reconstruct their *kofte* in the 1980s, they had to go to the Norwegian Folk Museum in Oslo to find the model.

It is the Coast Såmi who constitute the greater part of the Såmi population in Finnmark: 75 per cent in the census of 1930. By 1950 there were hardly any of them who would admit their origin. They were the ones who were exposed to the most brutal Norwegianization and have suffered the harshest fate. Once they regarded themselves as the true Såmi. Trappers, fishermen and small farmers, they lived off the resources the coast had to offer. Trade with Russia meant a great deal to them and kept them self-sufficient, but this ceased after the Russian Revolution. Then came the motorboat that needed capital investment and made their fishing methods obsolete. Finally there was the Second World War, when Finnmark was burnt and their entire existence disrupted.

What does the future hold in store for these people? At the end of the 1980s a Norwegian national newspaper used the original Såmi place names for the first time: Gaivoudna for Kåfjord, Deatnu for Tana. In 1987 these names were used when local authorities issued job advertisements: *Guovdageaidnu Suohkan* it said (Kautokeino Council), with a Lapp tent in its coat of arms. The Church, which from time to time has shown a positive attitude to the Såmi language, has bilingual services in

Nesseby, Tana, Karasjok and Kautokeino, and sometimes in other parishes. It is on the cards that Såmi will be the official language of most central Såmi councils, and Kautokeino already favours employing applicants with a knowledge of the language.

In 1855 half the population of Finnmark spoke Såmi. Today less than 10 per cent in the county speak this ancient language, which has 100 words for reindeer but none for war. How is it to survive the onslaught of the media?

Såmi Radio is of course a good means of communication. Part of the national network of the Norsk Rikskringkasting, it puts out daily news bulletins in Såmi in the north and in the capital. Nearly twice as many Såmi live in Oslo as in Karasjok and Kautokeino! The radio provides the only link with the outer world for the nomadic Såmi, and there was a great response to the information service introduced in 1987 which gave the Såmi the opportunity to ring in and warn other families if the reindeer track was so bad that the animals should be herded by a different route. Yet the Reindeer Såmi constitute less than one tenth of the total Såmi population. The Såmi Radio station in Karasjok also puts out a news programme in Norwegian to give listeners all over the country some idea of what is happening in the Såmi areas. In addition, it is supposed to produce TV programmes for the national network, but lacks money to make more than a couple a year. Såmi children have to learn Norwegian if they are to understand children's television at all.

There is no great tradition in written Såmi. An alphabet was published in Sweden in 1619, and Luther's Catechism in North Såmi and Norwegian in 1728. All told, there can be no more than a thousand books and publications in the language. Some Såmi authors have published their works in Norwegian. Among the first was Matti Aikio, with his realistic stories from the turn of the century. Now we have the poet Ailo Gaup and the novelist Annok Sarri Nordrå. In 1987 Ole Henrik Magga from Kautokeino presented the first doctoral dissertation in the Såmi language at the University of Oslo. That was where he was taught for the first time in his own mother tongue!

There is a Såmi newspaper in Karsjok, *Såmi Aigi*, and in the 80s, Såmi publishers were printing books for Såmi children in their own language.

An internationally acclaimed manifestation of the Såmi spirit was the first full-length Såmi film *Ofelav (The Pathfinder)*, made by Nils Gaup in 1987, about a band of maurauders who preyed on the Såmi in the Viking era. This film, nominated for an Oscar award, had the suspense of a modern action thriller combined with elements from the Såmi world of beliefs and imagination. Many of its actors came from the Såmi theatre group Beaiccas (The Sun), founded in Kautokeino in 1979.

The *joik*, the Såmi folksong, has enjoyed a renaissance through composers of modern music like John Persen, and through the outstanding Såmi folk singer Mari Boine Persen and her interpretations with jazz musicians such as the world-famous tenor saxophonist Jan Garbarek.

Yet not all Såmi dare admit to their culture. In 1987 Kautokeino Council tried to introduce an official *joik*, just as other boroughs have their town or city song, but colonial power still held sway. The same year this age-old, traditional mode of singing was still forbidden by law in Såmi schools.

No one can say that Norway's imperialist policy towards Såmiid Ædnan has not been successful.

THE MONARCHY

CHAPTER FIVE is about the Norwegian royal house and particularly about King Olav V who died in January 1991, aged 87, a monarch who was born with his skis on.

On the winter evening when the announcement was broadcast that the old king was dead, the people of Oslo started to gather outside the royal palace. With them they brought candles and flowers that they silently placed in the snow in the palace square. During the whole of the vigil the wintery square glowed with light and colour as the people mourned their dead king. And this scene repeated itself every night until after the funeral.

On the old king's death his only son, Crown Prince Harald, automatically became Harald V. At his side was Crown Princess Sonja, born a commoner, the daughter of an Oslo merchant, and now the country's new queen. There is no longer any coronation ceremony, and the only formal occasion that marked the transition from one reign to the next was the new monarch's reception in the Storting, Norway's national assembly, where he pledged an oath of loyalty to the Constitution.

There are few republicans in Norway, and even the most fervent of these bore no ill-will towards the old king himself. When he arrived at the annual Holmenkollen ski-jumping contest, a comfortable, elderly gentleman in blue plus-fours, knitted stockings, old-fashioned blue anorak and peaked cap with the emblem of the ski association, it was a signal to the whole country that the most important winter festival had started. That keen skiing enthusiast would then bring out pencil and paper to note down the scores, in total disregard of computer screens and other modern contraptions. Was he not after all a fully qualified judge? Had he not jumped at Holmenkollen in 1922 and 1923, and attended the competition almost uninterruptedly since 1911?

No wonder he was the favourite of ski-mad Norwegians. They sing 'God save our gracious King', forgetting that it is an imported anthem. Nor is the present Norwegian monarchy of long standing. For centuries we were subjects of foreign monarchs. There were no descendants of the Norwegian line left when the present monarchy was introduced in 1905, so a Danish prince, married to his English cousin, was brought over to our royal palace. The palace was not particularly grand either, as it had been intended as a guest residence for the Swedish king. It should in fact have been much larger; the idea was for an H-shaped building, but through lack of funds it ended up as a U. Even that was not completed until 1849.

Swedes, who have seen much grander things, tend to laugh at our palace, but we think it looks quite good on the hilltop above the city's main street. And if it makes the Swedes feel better, they can console themselves with the fact that it is Karl Johan, king of the Swedish/Norwegian union, who is mounted on a bronze charger and surveys the avenue that has been give his name.

The Danish prince, Carl, and his English princess, Maud, came here in 1905, after he had been elected King Haakon VII in a plebiscite. As sovereign he wielded little actual power, but was held in great respect. In a seafaring nation it may have helped towards his popularity that King Haakon VII had been a sailor himself and had tattoos on his arm. It was during wartime exile in London that he really became the people's king, a symbol of resistance to German occupation. A photograph that has become part of our history shows him and his son, Crown Prince Olav, under a birch tree in Molde during the dramatic flight of 1940. (Queen Maud had died in 1938.) At home in Norway small boys carved his initials between Nazi posters — an H with a 7 in it. When he came back to the capital after the war, on 7 June 1945, there was a rejoicing in Oslo such as had never been seen or heard before.

By then Crown Prince Olav had already returned to the country as chief of defence. As a fully trained officer he was well prepared for the task. From the age of eighteen he had participated in cabinet meetings, and during the war he had pleaded Norway's cause in Britain, just as the Swedish-born Crown Princess Märtha had done in the U.S.A., to which she had escaped with the children, Ragnhild, Astrid and Harald.

Crown Princess Märtha died in 1954, and when King Haakon was taken ill in 1955, Crown Prince Olav was appointed regent. On his father's death two years later, he ascended the throne with the same motto: 'Everything for Norway'.

We had had Olavs as kings before, dating back to the time when Harald Hairfaired united the kingdom of Norway. There were Olavs who converted the country to Christianity so that heads were rolling in all directions, Olavs who excelled as sportsmen. Olav V was one of the latter. However, unlike Olav Tryggvason, who ran on the oars while his men were rowing, Olav V preferred to stay inside the boat and win Olympic medals and other coveted sailing trophies.

He himself handed out royal trophies to the sportsmen of the year, and always turned up at the annual ski marathon, Birkebeineren, commemorating the time eight hundred years ago when his predecessor, King Haakon Haakonsson, was carried as a child by skiers over the mountains from Lillehammer to Rena. There are 5,700 participants who ski the 55 kilometres (34 miles) of blood, sweat and blisters. In 1994 the entire skiing world will compete in the surroundings of Lillehammer — during the Olympic Winter Games.

In his book The Final Testament of 1974, the outspoken Russian Premier Nikita Khrushchev provides some amusing descriptions of his visit to the king in 1964:

"We then travelled to Norway, which is also a monarchy. Of course I paid my respects to the Norwegian sovereign. I had been told that his late father had had such a strong belief in democracy that he used to take the tram to a place where he liked to fish, and that the other passengers often mistook him for an ordinary citizen. I'm not absolutely certain it is true that he behaved so democratically, but this was the story.

"I had been prepared for my meeting with the king, for he had

66

66. The char with its tomato-coloured belly is a tempting catch for the ice fisherman, who lies flat on the ice, peering down through the hole, waiting to strike at the right moment. (Dag Kjelsaas/NN/Samfoto)

67. Fishing through a hole in the ice of a lake is an activity that attracts Norwegians of all ages, especially in March and April, when the sun begins to warm. (Rolf Sørensen/NN/Samfoto)

68. Sailing has a long tradition in Norway, and various types of small sailing boat are owned by people from all walks of life. (A. O. Gautestad/NN)

69. Norway's new monarch, King Harald V, has honourably maintained the sailing traditions of the Norwegian royal family. The king has taken part in regattas in many waters of the world, and won the One Ton Cup for ocean racing at Kiel in the late 1980s. (Knudsens Fotosenter)

70

70. *It usually takes two to land a big salmon. Norway has several hundred rivers and streams where this fish comes to spawn. For many of them, fishing permits can be bought at a reasonable price.* (Tore Wuttudal/NN/ Samfoto)

71. All along the coast, but especially in western and northern Norway, there are rivers were salmon come to spawn and where anglers from far and near come to try their skill and luck. (Husmo-Foto)

72. On the rocky summit of Galdhøpiggen, hikers can find shelter in huts built mainly from local materials. (O. D. Enersen/Samfoto/NN)

73. When winter sets in, marinas and harbours become quiet, almost deserted places. The boats and their owners hibernate, waiting for the spring and warmer days to return. (Helge Sunde/Samfoto)

74. In the blue twilight of late summer, lamps shine warmly behind small windowpanes in bays and coves along the south coast. In the old days, a fisherman probably lived here; today it has become the holidaymaker's haven. (Kim Hart/Samfoto)

75

75. At Misje, on one of the islands lying off Bergen, brightly painted boat-houses give the place a lively look. Pleasure craft tend to predominate among the smaller vessels.
(R. Frislio/NN)

76. Innumerable lakes and rivers offer
many forms of outdoor activity in
summer. Canoeing is now one of the
most popular. The picture shows Lake
Femunden, the third biggest in
Norway, lying 670 metres (2,190 feet)
above sea level. (O. D. Enersen/
Samfoto/NN)

77. *The long-established spartan form of outdoor life, camping deep in the wilderness, still has many loyal followers, but their equipment has become more colourful.* (B. Areklett/ Samfoto/NN)

78. *The mountain is the great arena of outdoor life all year round. You do not even have to miss your daily bath: the shower under the waterfall is for free.* (Ola Røe/Samfoto)

rather a strange physical defect. My advisors said that he could begin laughing out loud for no apparent reason. He did not laugh because there was anything amusing, he just had this peculiarity or disease. If he were to start laughing in my presence, I must therefore take no notice – as if I had not heard it.

"We were driven to a building that did not look like a palace at all. There was nothing royal about it. It could not be compared with the palaces of our czars which I have visited in Leningrad and Peterhof, not least the palace of Catherine the Great, or of Paul at Tsarskoe Selo. The Norwegian palace looked like the house of any successful capitalist. At the door we were greeted by a man in a kind of khaki-coloured uniform. He ushered me into an office, showed me to a chair, and we sat down. Suddenly it occurred to me that this was the king. One could easily have mistaken him for the gardener," said Nikita Khrushchev.

What Khrushchev perhaps did not realize is that Olav was by no means impecunious. On the contrary, he was one of the richest men in Norway, second only to Olav Thon, who went to Oslo from Hallingdal after the war to sell fox pelts and ended up as the largest property owner in the country – worth two billion kroner in 1987. The Oslo paper *Dagbladet* estimated that Olav was worth one billion, after assessing his wealth and property in 1987. The Norwegian royal family therefore ranks as the sixth richest in Europe, wealthier than those of Sweden and Denmark, but unable to compete with the British monarchy, whose fortune is reckoned to be 22 billion kroner, according to the British expert H. B. Brooks-Baker in *Burke's Peerage*.

The Norwegian monarch owns estates in the United Kingdom worth 660 million kroner, left by Queen Maud. In Norway he owns Kongeseteren, the fairytale castle in Nordmarka that was part of the gift of the Norwegian people to King Haakon on his coronation in 1905. This was where King Olav resided during the skiing festival in Holmenkollen, and it was here that he died after suffering a heart atack. There is also Prinsehytta, the royal chalet in Jotunheimen, a gift from the Swedish king to Olav when he came of age. Olav himself bought a summer house, Bloksberg, near Hankø, for the sailing, but in his later years stayed on board the royal yacht when taking part in regattas.

The monarch's property also includes the extraordinary Solstraaleø (Sunshine Isle), in Sunnhordaland, a gift from the English family of Musgrove which fell out of favour with British royalty in Victorian times and settled in Norway. The island, though, is overgrown and seldom visited.

The palace, the summer residence at Bygdøy, Oscarshall castle on the Oslo fjord, the manor of Ledaal near Stavanger, Gamlehaugen near Bergen and Stiftsgården in Trondheim, where the king stays on his visits,. all these are owned by the State.

The late King Olav also held shares to the total value of more than five million kroner in a number of leading Swedish concerns. For his duties as king he received 8.4 million kroner from the Civil List in 1987. Of this 60 percent went on salaries for staff, and much of the remainder was used for official occasions and the upkeep of property.

As the son of a seaman and a keen sailor himself, King Olav had an especially weak spot for the royal yacht *Norge*, a gift from the Norwegian people on his 75th birthday in 1947. She was originally a luxury yacht called *Philante*, built for the British aeroplane magnate Sopwith in 1937. During the war the ship was on active service for three years.

79. Hang-gliding over Ringerike, north of Oslo. This peaceful yet exhilarating way of flying, taking off from mountain peaks or steep hillsides, now has many devotees. (Helge Sunde/Samfoto)

King Olav's three children all married commoners. Ragnhild, the eldest, is married to a shipowner's son and industrial magnate in Brazil, Erling S. Lorentzen. The second daughter, Astrid, is the wife of an Oslo businessman, Johan B. Ferner. Both princesses live relatively quiet lives away from the glare of the media.

The new royal couple, King Harald and Queen Sonja, both born in 1937, were married in 1968. When Harald saw the light of day, he was the first Norwegian prince to be born in the country since 1370. He was the youngest of King Olav's children, but he inherited the throne, for conservative Norway has not got around to introducing equal rights with regard to royalty.

Unperturbed by the fact that there are female monarchs in both England and Denmark, the Norwegian Constitution until recently stated:

"The line of succession is lineal and agnatic, so that only the legitimate male issue of a male may inherit."

There is every indication that King Harald was made aware of the necessary qualifications for being a Norwegian monarch when very young. At the ripe age of three he appeared at Holmenkollen for the first time. At the age of six he was sent into exile in America, where he refused to go to the barber's or have his hair cut; he was to be the new Harald Hairfaired who would save Norway! He returned to Norway with the royal family on 7 June 1945, and followed in his father's footsteps, being educated at Oxford, and in the army at home, becoming both general and admiral. We shall have to wait some time before we see a conscientious objector on the throne!

Whilst a royal bachelor, Harald naturally kept the press in business, and he was married off to quite a few princesses in his time. However, he himself chose a young girl from a department store in Oslo, Sonja Haraldsen. It is not clear whether this accorded with his father's wishes. The outspoken Jens Haugland, former minister of justice, wrote in his diary that 'the King asked Trygve Lie to speak to Crown Prince Harald and get him to marry according to his rank', but the former Secretary General of the United Nations refused to become involved.

Medieval abbey seals.

After a glorious royal wedding in 1968, the couple settled at Skaugum, a large farm in Asker outside Oslo, given to King Olav as a wedding present by Norway's ambassador in Spain, Fritz Wedel Jarlsberg. It is a farm of 100 acres of cultivated land, some 50 acres of pastureland, and some not too profitable forests. There is a staff of 20, which includes four footmen. As king and queen, they continue to live on the farm.

The royal couple have two children, Märtha Louise, born in 1971, and Haakon Magnus, born in 1973. Both perform folk dances merrily, and represent the royal family in a way that touches all hearts. Of the two it is again the younger, the boy, who will inherit the throne. In 1990 Parliament decided to change the Constitution in order to legalize female succession, but made it clear that the existing order should be kept for Prince Haakon Magnus.

How did Norway receive a queen who had no blue blood in her veins? They have taken her to their hearts, according to the popular press. It is universally agreed that they are an easy democratic couple. Harald is a good yachtsman like his father, a keen fisherman and a good shot, working at improving his performance with grouse shooting courses. The new queen is an outdoor girl and a good skier, who has competed incognito in the most strenuous of races, such as the Holmenkollen ski marathon. No wonder she is accepted in a skiing country!

WOMANPOWER

CHAPTER SIX is about the liberated Norwegian woman, about the Viking Frøydis who whetted her sword on her breasts, and about Prime Minister Gro Harlem Brundtland who formed a world-record-breaking women's cabinet.

It caused quite an international stir when doctor and politician Gro Harlem Brundtland in 1986 formed a minority government for the Norwegian Labour Party. Eight of the 18 ministers were women, herself included. She had held the office once before, serving as Norway's first women prime minister for some months in 1981. But at that time she had only three female cabinet ministers, and created more of a sensation by introducing academics into the Labour Party leadership. As a qualified physician, and the daughter of a doctor and former cabinet minister, she signalled the beginning of the end of a long tradition of working-class Labour Party politicians who derived their learning from the university of life. Thanks to her exceedingly hasty temper, revealed both on and off the air, the press was soon calling her 'the Harridan of Bygdøy', a nickname that gave vent to a good deal of male chauvinism on the part of political commentators. Bygdøy, where she lives, is incidentally one of the most desirable parts of Oslo.

Norwegians could with great satisfaction watch her take her place as the leading Nordic politician on the world stage.

She is not the first women to sort things out for the men! While by no means wanting to compare their methods, we ought perhaps to mention what Eric the Red's daughter Frøydis did when she met the *Skrælingers* in Vinland and her male companions' courage failed:

"Frøydis came out and saw Karlsevne and his men running away. She cried: 'Why are you fleeing from these miserable creatures? I would have thought that great fellows like you could knock them down like cattle! If I only had a weapon, I believe I would fight better than any of you!' But they did not heed what she said. Frøydis ran after them, but was too slow as she was with child. She followed the others into the woods, but the *Skrælingers* were behind her. She found a dead man in the wood. It was Torbrand Snorreson, with a stone lodged in his skull. Beside him lay his sword, and she raised it to defend herself. As the *Skrælingers* approached, she uncovered her breasts and whetted her sword on them."

The saga of Eric the Red recounts that the natives were so horrified they ran to their boats and rowed away!

Experts differ in their opinions as to the real condition of Norwegian women at this time of expansion for the country. Of course the sagas mostly tell us about upper-class women: queens, and the wives and daughters of chieftains. Seven hundred years before the Viking era, the Roman historian Tacitus wrote that 'the women follow their men into battle, caring for the wounded'. He was amazed that so many women mastered runes, and he was surprised by the sexual morality of the Nordic barbarians, who held that a girl without her virginity was disgraced, and by the mutual respect between men and women. Snorre Sturlason, the Icelandic saga-writer, names many wise and capable women, but only one who spoke up in the council.

The Viking era was the foremost age of slavery in Norwegian history. Many of the estimated 75,000 slaves were brought home as booty after raids. One of the Edda poems from this time, *Rigstula*, gives

Edvard Munch: Sitting Nude, 1896, charcoal, pencil and watercolour.

us a picture of Tir, a woman slave, arriving at the farm with muddy boots, sunburnt arms and a hooked nose. It then describes how she baked flat bread. The Arabian writer and explorer Ahmed ibn Fadlan tells us that the Nordic Vikings in Russia had many women slaves about them. Sometimes these were burnt with orgiastic ritual on the funeral pyre of their deceased lord. That female slaves were sacrificed and placed at their queen's side we know from the Oseberg ship, the Viking vessel found in Vestfold and now to be seen at Bygdøy in Oslo. A woman slave could be given away, sold, hired out, and even killed by her owner without it being considered murder in the eyes of the law. If she stole anything worth even one øre, she was to have one ear cut off. On repeating the offence, she lost the other. At the third offence she lost her nose. A woman slave who had given birth was let off work until she was strong enough to carry two buckets of water from the well.

The battle for women's rights in Norway started in the middle of the nineteenth century, inspired partly by the novel *Amtmannens Døtre* by Camilla Collett, sister of the rebel poet Henrik Wergeland. For women of the middle class it was important to secure the right to education, while for working-class women it was more important to be able to make a living and to limit the number of pregnancies. For both these groups the aim was to get the vote – achieved in 1913, fifteen years after universal suffrage for men.

The great wave of women's liberation that swept through the western world in the 1970s made a clear impact in Norway. As in other places it was a two-pronged movement, driven by the 'New Feminists', who emphasized the raising of women's consciousness at all levels, including the sexual, while the more Marxist 'Women's Front' concentrated on the economic aspect, their banners proclaiming: 'No class struggle without female struggle, no female struggle without class struggle.' Both factions fought for equal rights in every area, with specific demands for more crèches, the right to abortion, equal opportunities in education, equal pay for equal work.

When Gro Harlem Brundtland formed her 'women's cabinet' in 1986, it was part of a long process that is still not complete. Norway could have had women cabinet ministers as early as 1916, and yet it was not until 1945 that the first, the Communist Kirsten Hansteen, took office. Most of Harlem Brundtland's female ministers were in charge of areas of special interest to women, such as education, health, law, the environment, consumer affairs and overseas aid. The toughest job was perhaps the one given to Gunhild Øyangen, arts graduate and farmer's wife from Trøndelag, who was placed in charge of the traditionally male-dominated Ministry of Agriculture.

If you look at the way jobs and elected offices are distributed in Norway, you will still see a clear male domination. In 1987 only one in four councillors was female. Out of the two million employed in the country, only 44 per cent are women, most of them in typically female jobs. This is also reflected in their wages. Men still earn more than women, despite the accepted principle of equal pay for equal work. Men get the top jobs, and they make all the major decisions, even in 'female' occupations. In the postal service, for instance, more women are employed than men. Yet there is no female director, and there are only four women among the country's 135 postmasters. A mere four per cent of professors in Norway are women, only 10 per cent of the civil servants in the police force, only 16 per cent of self-employed persons in business. Only 27 per cent of the girls who have the right to inherit a farm are certain that they will indeed take it over.

Girls still prefer the traditional female occupations, according to a survey carried out by the University of Trondheim. They want to be 1) hairdressers or beauticians, 2) tourist guides, 3) hospital nurses, 4) children's nurses, 5) veterinary surgeons, 6) cooks, 7) physicians, 8) civil engineers and engineers, 9) lawyers, 10) computer operators.

Boys on the other hand want to be 1) mechanics, 2) engineers, 3) farmers, 4) pilots, 5) computer operators, 6) electricians, 7) carpenters, 8) cooks, 9) directors or managers, 10) policemen.

There is some light in the gloom. More women than men continue with further education beyond secondary school: 40 per cent of women and 25 per cent of men. The percentage of women in the male-dominated colleges has doubled in recent years and is now 42 at the National College of Agricultural Engineering, 33 at the College of Business Administration and Economics, and 24 at Norway's College of Technology.

Some women have broken down barriers and made Norwegian history. In 1961 Ingrid Bjerkaas was ordained as Norway's first woman minister of the Church of Norway. In 1968 Lily Bølviken became the first

Poster by Edvard Munch for Henrik Ibsen's 'Peer Gynt', Paris 1896.

woman High Court judge. In 1974 Ebba Lodden became regional commissioner, and was thus the most important 'man' in the county. In 1987 Siri Skare became Norway's first woman Air Force pilot, though she was not permitted to fly fighter planes. In the same year we find Ellen Holager Andenæs in charge of the uniformed branch of the Oslo police, and Ellen Stensrud elected as the first woman leader of the powerful, male-dominated Oslo Engineering Workers' Union, the largest in the country with 13,000 members.

In recent years it is mostly women who have put Norway on the map in the field of sport. These include marathon runners Grete Waitz and Ingrid Kristiansen, and the women's national handball and soccer teams.

The most entrenched opposition to equal rights for women is to be found in the Church and in Christian organizations. Members of the clergy have carried out boycott action if a female minister officiates, and a female resident curate was prevented from conducting the Christmas service because the male organist refused to play. The mighty Norwegian Lutheran Home Mission Society is against women priests as 'contrary to the Word of God', and there are still bishops in the Norwegian Church who refuse to ordain women priests. But attitudes in general have changed. Just after the Second World War almost half the population was against women priests, while today 90 per cent are in favour. So it is really only a question of time before the first woman bishop takes up her crozier.

In 1978 the first Equal Rights Law was passed, banning discrimination in the treatment of men and women. The following year the equal rights Ombudsman, Eva Kolstad, was appointed to see that the law was carried out, for instance in matters of employment. Farm girls have changed the ancient system of odal tenure of land and the allodial law so that now it is the eldest child who inherits a farm, not necessarily the eldest boy, as before.

A new abortion law gives women the right to take the final decision on terminating a pregnancy. The law on names has also been changed, so that a baby born in Norway today is automatically given the mother's family name. If the parents wish the child to have the father's name, they must specifically state this.

In 1981 the world's first children's Ombudsman was appointed, whose job it is to see that children's rights are respected. A law passed in 1987 forbids adults to perform any act of violence towards children. It states that spanking and clips over the ear are forbidden, though light, reprimanding smacking is permitted — but it is not quite clear how you are to distinguish between the two.

In recent years the struggle against pornography, abuse of women, incest and rape have been dominant female issues in Norway. There are 50 centres for battered women in the country, and the Oslo health board runs a reception centre for rape victims.

The Norwegian woman is not out of the urban mould, accustomed to ball-gowns, powder puffs and smelling salts. She has been formed by hard labour, on the coast, high in the mountains, and on steep hillsides — not the kind to swoon, or wilt in the face of adversity.

"They are all dressed in black. The men's costume is not distinguished other than by some large buttons similar to those worn by our lackeys, but the women wear a hideous skirt that barely reaches the knee. It clings tightly around the hips and has a great many pleats at the

80. The North Sea oil industry introduced the supply ship as a new type of vessel in the Norwegian merchant marine. (Husmo-Foto)

bottom, not unlike the wide pantaloons worn by Dutch seamen. If our *Parisiennes* had had such garments, they would have had no need of all the transparent materials so fashionable of late. They are as revealing of the body's contours as if they had been naked. And yet I will insist on this being the most unattractive garment I have ever seen," our friend Jacques de la Tocnaye reported from Trøndelag in 1799.

Other aspects of Norwegian life seem to have appealed more to this somewhat narrow-minded officer. He writes of west Norway:

"The women prepare the food. The men say grace and sit down in a corner where they eat their fill in peace and quiet. When they have finished the women sit down in another corner and eat whatever is left over. I will not maintain that this is particularly gallant behaviour, but it does prove again that Norwegian women, with the exception of those in Trondheim and Christiania (Oslo), know how to accord their husbands the respect due to them."

So things must have made some progress in the course of two centuries. However, the concept of equal rights is probably not uppermost in everyday life. In most homes it is the woman who does the cooking, though the husband may undertake some domestic chores. It is remarkable how many homes installed dishwashers as soon as the male took his place at the kitchen sink! And it is not only in the urban homes of intellectuals that we see a new division of labour. In the country it was customary for the woman to have sole responsibility for the cows and milking. It was considered degrading for the husband to go into the cowshed. Today men and women share most of the work. Yet our antiquated legal system will not acknowledge this. In 1987 a court ruled that a farmer's earnings were greater than his wife's, the reason being that he could also drive a tractor!

It is not possible to give a single description that covers all Norwegian women of today. They are as varied as the landscape. There is an ocean of difference in attitude, life style and experience between the fisherman's wife working with bait in a Lofoten fishery and the office girl at her computer in fashionable Bygdøy Allé in Oslo.

Southern Europeans do not distinguish between different Scandinavian women, but lump them all together. This may have started with the Nordic woman as portrayed in the films of Ingmar Bergman and other Swedish film directors of the 50s: beautiful blonde girls who danced through the summer, frankly proclaming their sexuality.

But of course there is a difference between the women, as there is between all the people of Scandinavia. The Norwegian woman never became feminist in the same way as the Danish. She did not spend her summers in women's camps, or discuss her sex life openly with journalists, or even in private. Nor does the Norwegian woman organize her life as meticulously and rationally as the Swedish woman seems to do, in everything from vegetarian food to sexual diet.

Above all the Norwegian girl is a friend and a comrade, whether she lives in a town or in the country, by the coast or in the mountains. It is therefore strange that she has stepped out of the traditional female role well known from more southerly countries, where the woman sacrifices herself for her parents-in-law and does not consign them to an old people's home. It may be a weakness in Norwegian social democracy, or it may be a sign of strength. Perhaps it is an indication that we are only half-way along our road to social welfare: the new woman has fulfilled herself, the old woman has been left out in the final reckoning.

81. The fishing boats that go out after cod in late winter often have to contend with rough seas. (Husmo-Foto) ▷

82. Seagulls accompany the fishing vessels like a living cloud. To a large extent they depend on the 'goodies' that are wasted or discarded by the fishermen. (Husmo-Foto) ▷ ▷

83. Besides operating in its coastal waters, the Norwegian fishing fleet engages in seasonal fishing in the Arctic, around Bear Island, for instance, where this picture was taken. (Husmo-Foto) ▷ ▷ ▷

84. The area of the Lofoten
archipelago, with spawning cod
beneath the glittering surface and
snowclad mountains reaching skyward,
is as attractive for painters as it is for
fishermen. (Husmo-Foto)

85. Most of the Norwegian fishing
fleet consists of small, but very
seaworthy boats. (Husmo-Foto)

86. The fish market, which begins where the harbour ends, offers the Bergen housewife live fish and other delicacies from the sea. (Helge Sunde)

87. The capelin, a small fish of the smelt family, is very important for Norwegian fisheries: when the capelin approaches the shore to spawn, the cod follows. In addition, this fish is an important resource of the fishing industry in its own right. (Husmo-Foto)

88. During the main fishing season, in late winter and early spring, vessels from many parts of the country converge on Lofoten. (Hugo Henriksen/Samfoto)

89

90

89. *Far out at sea, beyond the Lofoten archipelago in northern Norway, lies the small community of Røst with its multitude of islets, many of them famous for their colonies of sea birds.* (Hans Hvide Bang/Samfoto/NN)

90. *A large proportion of the goods transported in Norway is carried by boat. Small cargo vessels are a common sight among the thousands of skerries and isles scattered off the coast.* (R. Frislid/NN)

91. *A summer's night in the north with the light of the midnight sun shining on distant mountains: Lyngen fjord backed by the Lyngen Alps.* (R. Frislid/NN)

92. With all its fjords and bays and inlets, the Norwegian coastland has a total length of 21,000 kilometres (13,000 miles). Everywhere along the shore fishing boats, big and small, are a feature of the scene. (R. Frislid/NN)

93. The flat North Cape plateau, high above the ice-cold Polar Sea, teems with tourists all summer. The elongated promontory of Knivskjellodden (in the foreground) stretches even farther north than the North Cape. (Husmo-Foto)

SEASONS AND CELEBRATIONS

*CHAPTER SEVEN relates what Kari and Ola do
with themselves all year round, when, what and
how they celebrate, and what they like to drink.*

What exactly do Kari and Ola Nordmann do up there under the glacier all the year? What do they get up to? What do they celebrate? Let's start with the winter straight away and get it over and done with.

Even if Ola Nordmann has by now 10,000 years of experience of the snow, he is caught off guard every single year. People in the mountainous regions are not really taken by surprise; they have a natural relationship with both snow and ice and take them as they come – sometime in early autumn.

But when the snow has settled inland for about a month, a strange thing happens. It starts snowing near the coast, where the journalists live and where the newspapers are printed. What a sensation! The dramatic headlines totally ignore the inland areas. 'Winter has set in! Total chaos on the roads! Snowploughs caught in blizzard!' And indeed there are long traffic jams with cars that won't start and petrol stations that have run out of tow ropes and are besieged by people who have decided to change from summer to winter tyres. In Norway it is normal to use studded tyres in winter, something visiting Danes forget, which leaves them standing at the bottom of the hills, blocking the road with their lorries. Studded tyres wear out the asphalt and make a mess of the surroundings, but they do save lives.

When it has finished snowing, it is time for the cold weather to set in. And there is nothing whatsoever to be said in favour of a Norwegian winter when the temperature sinks to minus 30° C or lower. There are some places that always have the record for the coldest temperatures, for instance Østerdalen and inland Finnmark. Yet it can feel just as cold at minus 20° C on the wet and stormy coastline as at 40° below zero in the still winter landscape of mountainous Røros.

The effects are the same. When you want to start the car to let the snowplough through you discover that the lock is frozen so you can't get in, the bonnet won't open, the batteries are flat, and the windscreen is impossible to see through. In the houses the pipes freeze, lavatories are blocked, and in draughty buildings old people have to stay in bed to keep warm. 'Log angels' deliver free firewood to the elderly, construction workers are made redundant, forestry work ceases, railway points freeze, mountain passes are closed, ships weighed down by ice have to seek a harbour. Even the Oslo fjord sometimes freezes over, so that you

94. The narrow fjords of western Norway, with their steep sides and waterfalls plunging into the sea, are among the most popular destinations of foreign tourists. This picture is from Geiranger fjord. (Husmo-Foto)

can walk right out to sea, where the icebreaker struggles to clear a shipping lane.

At this point extraordinary things can happen. While the whole of southern Norway is stamping its feet to keep warm, we hear that the temperature has made a leap above zero on Svalbard, the island jammed up against the North Pole. Northern Norway can experience a variation of temperature of up to 40 °C in the course of a day!

One gets used to everything – even winter. Kari prefers woollen undergarments and high boots to nylon tights and a weak bladder. The Norwegian winter is so beautiful, and snow is essential for Christmas, the greatest time of celebration for Norwegians. So Jacques de la Tocnaye discovered in 1799:

"At Christmastide the Norwegians like feasting and celebrating with their friends. To make it quite clear how hospitable they are and how essential it is that everyone is happy, they even set up a sheaf of oats on a pole outside the barn door, to give the birds something to eat. The sheaf remains hanging until it falls of its own accord, and no one would dream of using it to entice the birds so they could be caught and eaten." Only a French gourmet could voice such a thought!

The Christmas sheaves are still to be seen, hanging outside farmhouses and on the balcony of high-rise blocks, and the robin redbreast features in the sheaf on all the Christmas cards Norwegians send each other.

The festive season is well prepared for. By September the restaurants are trying to work up a Christmas appetite in their customers with firtree-shaped advertisements tempting them with 'Christmas sausage, Christmas ham, Christmas anchovies, Christmas pork, Christmas ale, etc., etc.' – in short, the legendary Christmas spread, *julebord*.

In the days before Christmas tension increases dramatically. Everything has to be ready by Christmas Eve. By then all cakes must be baked, all stars hung up in the windows and on the front door, and all gifts must be wrapped. The Norwegians have their main celebration on Christmas Eve. For many people it is the only day in the year when they go to church. It is the day when the whole family holds each other by the hand and proceeds round the tree singing the old familiar carols, while mother and father have tears in their eyes as they think back to the Christmases of their childhood.

But the Christmas tree is Danish! In Norway, land of forests, 30 per cent of the one million or so Christmas trees sold are imported from Denmark, despite the fact that they are twice as expensive as the Norwegian ones. The reason is that the Danes have managed to grow a tree that does not shed its needles as easily as the untidier domestic product. So in the past ten years the Danes have captured a large chunk of the Norwegian Christmas-tree market. Yet forestry research is being carried out, and there is hope that one day the honour of the country may be restored. In any case, many of the Norwegian Christmas hymns are also of Danish origin.

Father Christmas, however, is Norwegian. At least so children from all over the world believe, to judge from the letters that get sent to the Chief Tourist Officer in Oslo.

Christmas dinner is highly traditional, but varies according to region. 'In the barn sits Father Christmas with his porridge' is one of the more popular seasonal songs. It was for long a custom to put out a plateful of porridge both in the festive season and at other times for

Father Christmas, or *Nissen.* He is not the large American-style Santa, but a small gnome-like, grey-bearded, homespun creature.

The usual Christmas Eve dinner in the east of Norway consists of roast pork, meat rissoles, sausages and sauerkraut, with cream of cloudberries or creamed rice for dessert. There is an almond hidden in the rice, which brings the lucky finder an extra gift. Beer and aquavit will be drunk, unless it is a teetotal family. In the west, the menu is salted and dried ribs of mutton, mashed swedes, potatoes, beer and aquavit. The meat will have been smoked over a layer of birch sprigs placed at the bottom of the pot. In the south many people eat steamed cod on Christmas Eve, accompanied by red wine. The special dish *lutefisk* is also served at Christmas time. This is made of dried cod prepared in a special potash lye, traditionally made from birch ash. It used to be said that the lye is particularly strong at Christmas if the wife is bad-tempered.

The Lapps eat saddle of reindeer at Christmas, served with white bread, a great rarity and delicacy in former times. But in our Norwegianized era both *lutefisk* and pork have invaded the homes of the Såmi.

Many take a holiday in the days between Christmas and New Year. On New Year's Eve the Norwegians let their hair down again. At midnight there is a carnival atmosphere in the ice-cold winter. Boats blow their horns in the harbour and people rush out into the winter night, onto their balconies or into the street — to let off fireworks to the tune of 100 million kroner. There are strict regulations about letting off rockets, and one is supposed to obtain a licence from the police. On New Year's Eve every Norwegian breaks the law.

The month of January closes with a somewhat more prosaic event, the filling in of the income-tax return form, the annual report to the tax authorities on how much you earned in the past year.

It is dark in Norway in winter, especially in the north, where the sun disappears completely below the horizon to make up for having stayed up all day and all night in the summer. The soul of the north Norwegian grows restless when the fantastic sunlight again appears on the horizon after the dark season. In Tromsø they celebrate 'Sun Day', and locals go up into the hills from where they can look to the south. People drink 'sun coffee' and eat cakes, the fire brigade provides hot chocolate, cream and buns for its men, while others exchange their usual packed lunch for Danish pastries and cocoa. Some of the more optimistic outdoor restaurants venture a pre-season opening. School children used to get the day off to celebrate the return of the sun. Now they have cocoa and buns and a carnival before running out at noon into the first spindly rays from the guest of honour peeping out between the peaks of Balsfjord.

The true Nordic sun worship is to be seen at Easter! After people have spent all winter shovelling snow, and the children have just exchanged their winter boots for shoes that allow them to lift their feet off the ground, you would think they would have had enough of winter. Far from it. The 10,000-year-old yearning for the glacier must still be in the Norseman's bones. Every Easter there is a mass migration when 800,000 Norwegians pack a thermos, sandwiches, oranges and a detective novel in their rucksack, bring out their skis and set off for the mountains. The Norwegian State Railway has its peak season, buses have their roofs piled high with skis, and the Red Cross and other bodies stand by with teams of 10,000 or more voluntary First Aid helpers, divers, glacier climbers, mountain rescue dogs, helicopters and planes, ready to save people who get lost or caught in avalanches on their holiday. Even so, help does not always arrive in time.

Every fourth household has a cottage in the mountains or by the sea. In addition, the Norwegian Tourist Association has huts scattered all over the country. The energetic have 16,000 kilometres (10,000 miles) of track to explore. In the Tourist Association huts there is always room, even if it means sleeping in the sauna. Many people spend their Easter holiday skiing from hut to hut. Often these are self-service, that is, the guests help themselves to the food they need and leave the money. No-one is around to check up on this — the Tourist Association trusts its members. Recently, however, there have been cases of non-payment, resulting in a loss of six to eight per cent every year, so the Association threatens to stop this unique tradition of Norwegian hospitality.

It has always been a status symbol to return from the Easter holiday with a tanned face. And however much of a welfare state Norway may be, Easter in the mountains is still for the healthy and — well-off. Predictably, statistics show that the larger a family's income, the more chance of them going away on holiday. Norway has the world's longest Easter break, with a public holiday on Maundy Thursday, Good Friday, half Saturday, and Easter Sunday and Monday. Those who stay at home can also enjoy solving crime mysteries, as for some extraordinary reason Easter and who-dunnits have become synonymous. There is always a thriller serialized on TV in Holy Week.

The fact that Norwegians are born with skis on has affected their behaviour at times other than at Easter.

Skis must have been in use in Siberia and in Europe about four or five thousand years ago. A Greek fifth-century source tells us of Lapps skiing, and the Norse sagas portray both heroes and heroines on skis. The goddess Skadi could shoot with her bow and arrow while on skis, which should give her the credit for having started the biathlon.

The oldest pairs consisted of one long and one short ski, the shorter being covered in hide to give a powerful kick. Skiing as a sport did not really get going until the appearance in the eighteenth century of the Telemark ski, which was narrow in the middle and had a raised tip. It was superseded by the laminated skis of the 1930s, and from 1970 all Norwegians have been born with plastic skis on. But there are still wooden skis to be seen, treasured by wooden-ski enthusiasts. who are looked upon as freaks when they appear on the slopes dressed in quaint knickerbockers. Young skiers of today look more like astronauts, equipped with special skis, special helmets and space suits from the age of

Snowcastle under attack. Illustration to Olaus Magnus 'History of the Nordic Peoples', Rome 1555.

three. However, the late 80s ushered in a nostalgic return to the old Telemark way of skiing.

The father of skiing as we know it, Sondre Norheim, came from Telemark, where his childhood home, in Morgedal, is today a museum. He taught people to ski in Norway and in the U.S.A., to which he emigrated in 1884. Another native of Telemark, Jon Torsteinson Rue, otherwise known as Snowshoe Thompson, became legendary in the last century when for twenty years he brought the mail on skis over the Sierra Nevada from Placerville in California to Virginia City in Nevada.

Our most famous ski hero is perhaps Fridtjof Nansen, the polar scientist, who skied over Greenland in 1888, and later tried to ski to the North Pole with his companion Hjalmar Johansen. After these two had spent a year together in the icy wastes, and saved each other's life more than once, Nansen went so far as to suggest that they should address each other by the familiar *du*, which should dispel the idea that Norwegians are a reserved people. Roald Amundsen was a hero of the same calibre, planting the Norwegian flag on the South Pole in 1911.

More attainable is the feat of Olaf Rye, who 180 years ago jumped 9.5 metres (30 feet) at Eidsborg, which must be reckoned as the first Norwegian ski-jumping record. Norwegians have always been very keen on jumping, provided they win. They usually did to begin with, when there were more modest requirements as to style and length.

The greatest winter sports event for Norwegians is the Holmenkollen competition, the jumping event that counts as our second national day. When the Olympic Games were held in Norway in 1952, there were 120,000 spectators at Holmenkollen. Every year Holmenkollen Sunday is a great festival, with tens of thousands of people going up there on foot or by tram, with a thermos in their rucksack, to the accompaniment of brass bands. From the tender age when Norwegians first toddle forth on small skis, the great dream is to win the jumping at Holmenkollen. The event gets tremendous media coverage, and the winner is a national hero — until the next year.

All winter long people take long ski trips, into the forests, over the mountains — a wonderful thing to do when snow crystals glitter and powder snow is scattered from the trees. Cross-country skiing events are popular all over the country, the Birkebeiner run being the most famous.

In recent years alpine skiing has become a national sport, for those who can afford the equipment. There are 500 ski lifts set up for the nation's 450,000 downhill skiers, in Hemsedal, at Geilo, in Voss, in Trysil, and many other places. Norwegians are not yet quite sure of themselves when it comes to this Continental fashion, so they have called the new ski resort near Oslo 'Norefjell *Alpine* Village'.

Skating was the great spectator sport in Norway for as long as Norwegians got the medals, especially when they won every time as they did with Hjalmar 'Hjallis' Andersen, gold-medallist in the 1952 Olympic Games. He will remain forever Norway's King of Skating, and Sonja Henie the Queen.

Spring comes late to this elongated country of ours. It is a melancholic season, when the people of Jaeren look out for the lapwing, when children play hopscotch, and the Minister of Transport announces special restrictions due to the frost. The frost sits deep in the ground, and the roads cannot take heavy loads in the spring thaw.

May Day is celebrated by the Labour movement in Norway, as in other countries. It is also the day when anti-socialists cause a good deal of irritation by not hoisting their flags and by demonstratively working on their farms or in the garden.

A day celebrated by everyone is 17 May – in honour of Norway's Constitution of 1814. There can be no other country in the world that celebrates its national day in such a manner. For days beforehand, brass bands can be heard in every school and on every street, practising patriotic songs and all the marches to be played in this otherwise unmilitary country. Now the red and the blue *Russ* make their noisy appearance, the thousands of students celebrating the end of twelve years of school with their specially painted red or blue cars, their ribald newspapers, their beerdrinking competitions, and their Miss Russ awards. The ones dressed in blue have attended commercial high school, the ones in red have graduated from other high schools.

At a very early hour small children start blowing their 17 May trumpets in the street and waving their flags. Foreign visitors are especially impressed by the children's procession in Oslo, when tens of thousands of schoolchildren with bands and flags parade up Karl Johan Street to greet the king on his balcony. The day provides an explosion of colour in this country of granite.

When Ola and Kari wake up from their winter hibernation they feel the need to get out into the garden. Norwegians love their gardens: 66 per cent of households have their own, 23 per cent have access to communal gardens, and only 11 per cent have to make do with balcony boxes.

Midsummer Night's Eve, 23 June, has been another great festivity for many hundreds of years. The old Frostating Law from the twelfth century prescribed how *Jonsok* was to be celebrated, and gave detailed instructions as to how the farmer should brew his St Hans or St John beer. On the coast, thousands of little boats go out to the small islands where huge bonfires are lit, and there is dancing to the accordion (or blaring rock music) until sunrise. A romantic calm descends on Ola and Kari Nordmann when the sea lies still and the birds briefly go to rest. Next morning they have a headache.

Soccer is the great spectator sport in the summer, although interest has dwindled somewhat in the past few years. Norwegian football is still in the transition stage between amateur and professional. The country insists on 'non-amateur' or semi-professional status, which means that players should, at least in theory, have a job that brings in more than they get from playing football. Yet Norwegian soccer has gone international and has to call on professionals from all over Europe when the national team is picked. There are now concrete plans to make the game fully professional.

Norway is above all a country that goes in for sports and athletic pursuits for the masses. Sports associations have 1.7 million members, more than one per household! There are many different mass meetings. The greatest soccer festival is the Norway Cup in Oslo, when 1,100 youth teams compete, among them guests from all over the world. In recent years mass running events have become popular: the Oslo Marathon with 8,000 competitors, the Oslo Centre Race that draws 12,000 participants, and others. The great trial of strength is the annual cycle race from Trondheim to Oslo. The fastest do the 554-kilometre (344-mile) stretch in 14 hours, the slowest take a couple of days. In addition mass walks are arranged all over the country.

In fact, walking, hiking or rambling, call it what you will – they call it a *tur* – is a Norwegian speciality. Every evening after the News, Kari and Ola go for a little stroll in the neighbourhood. Every weekend the woods and forests are filled with Norwegians with a knapsack and thermos flask, pushing the baby and with the dog on a lead. You name it, the Norwegians will have a *tur* for it: by car or boat, sailing, scouting, fishing, mountain climbing, a *tur* for Sunday and one for gathering every conceivable berry in the forest.

In July Kari and Ola go away for their annual vacation. They water their plants, lock the door, putting their boots outside to make burglars think they are at home, and forget their house or flat for the next three or four weeks. Many simply go to their family in the country, others go walking in the mountains or on a boating holiday to the south of Norway. In the Oslo fjord and in the south there is teeming life in the summer, when tens of thousands of people spend their holidays on board their boats or in the numerous camp sites along the coast. Many foreigners hire cabins in Norway. Keen anthropologists have calculated that 4,050 million nights were spent in private cabins in 1984, while only 11 million were spent in hotels.

But many people also go the opposite way, from the countryside to the cities. According to a Tourist Board list, the most popular attractions are the Vigelandsanlegget sculpture park and the Holmenkollen ski-jump area in Oslo, the Fløybanen climbing tramway in Bergen, the Tusenfryd amusement park, the Viking Museum and the Kon-Tiki Museum in Oslo, the Kristiansand animal park, and the Nidarosdomen Cathedral in Trondheim.

A large number of Norwegians prefer to go to southern climes in the summer – if they haven't already been there in the winter. Tour operators tempt the public with around 50 destinations in 20 countries, and 400,000 yearly succumb. Many go to the Canary Islands, where they find waiters who speak Norwegian – or at least Swedish. More and more opt to buy their own house in Spain or the South of France, especially pensioners fleeing from the Nordic winter.

One rather special 'package tour' is to 'Costa del Ilseng' near Hamar. Ilseng is a work camp for drunken drivers, many of whom spend their three-week 'holiday' on carpentry, assembling lamps, or wrapping cakes of soap, rather than drinking wine and eating grilled pork in Las Palmas. Around 7,000 Norwegians were sentenced for drunken driving in 1984. It has been reckoned that 200,000 drivers a year take to the road with 6.5 times more than the prescribed limit of alcohol (0.50) in the bloodstream. What else do we do in summer? Young people who have worked to save money in the first weeks of summer, go Inter-Railing at the end of the holiday. In 1986, 16,000 young people took advantage of this scheme for cut-price travel on the railways of Europe.

The bees buzz in the fields, the waves lap against the shore, a sleepy wind meanders through city streets, and the Norwegian summer goes by. A hectic strawberry season is followed by the blueberry season, when Kari and Ola are to be seen in the woods, heads down, bottoms up, snipping away with their special berry-pickers. Haymaking is followed by potato picking, and then one day there is a breath of autumn in the air, the trees turn yellow, and the leaves begin to fall.

The frost sets in the ground, it is hard underfoot, soon the first flakes of snow are swirling in the air, and Norwegians can once more let themselves be caught by surprise at the onset of winter – for the 10,001st time!

Whatever the season or cause for celebration, *Skål!* is the toast.

Foreigners are always immensely amused by Norwegian drinking laws. And one can't get away from the humour in laws that permit you to buy a whole crate of beer at the local store, but not one bottle on its own. Or when a local inhabitant is refused a drink on the terrace of the local hotel, while his good friend from the neighbouring town can order as much as he likes. This is the tail-end of a tradition of fighting the evils of alcoholism that was inaugurated a century ago by such pioneers Asbjørn Kloster, whose statue you can see in Stavanger – a campaign that meets with little enthusiasm today.

Norwegians have extraordinarily long and strong traditions in drinking and drunkenness. Snorre tells us that our great hero of Viking times, Olav Tryggvason, got people drunk so he could set fire to their houses if they refused to become Christians.

"They longed for the intoxicating drink as a bear longs for honey," runs another description of the Vikings, who would travel great distances in foreign parts in order to get wine while on their plundering trips to the Mediterranean. "Rich merchants live well and drink fairly heavily," wrote Jacques de la Tocnaye. Europeans must have learnt the art of distilling liquor some time after the end of the Viking period, but spirits were first introduced into Norway by Archhishop Olav Engelbrektsson in Trondheim in 1530. Once in the country, distilling apparatus became as normal a part of household equipment as pots and pans.

It just had to go wrong for the drink-crazy Norwegians. The battle against the Demon was launched in the middle of the sixteenth century, when it became forbidden to serve spirits (hard liquor) on Sundays and holidays – a law that stands to this day. Despite all regulations, people went on making spirits, first from grain, then from potatoes when they were introduced in the eighteenth century. At about that time distilling became illegal, though the law was repealed in 1816. Once more consumption increased dramatically, reaching 16 litres of spirits per citizen in 1833 (one litre = nearly two pints). It was this that led to the temperance movement.

In 1848 a law on the manufacture and processing of spirits put an end to home distilling. In its place legal, industrial distilling was established. Whereas in 1832 there were 10,000 registered distilleries in the country, a couple of decades later only 40 were left. The number of establishments licensed for the sale and serving of spirits was halved, and by 1851 the consumption of spirits had fallen to six litres per head.

From 1916 to 1927 prohibition was enforced, for some years including even fortified wine. Since 1922 the State has had a monopoly of the distribution and sale of wines and spirits in the country, and since 1927 over the production of spirits as well. Today six distilleries deliver spirits to the Wine Monopoly, about two million litres a year altogether. Some 2,000 farmers send potatoes to be distilled. The Wine Monopoly carries out production in Hamar, Oslo, Bergen and Trondheim, and runs 95 shops.

In latter years there has been a relaxation in alcohol legislation. It is still not possible to buy wine in the local store, as in Denmark and most other European countries. But whereas only half the population of Norway could buy beer in their own parish in 1955, this is now possible for 97.3 per cent of the population, and about 50 per cent live in areas that have a Wine Monopoly outlet.

What does Ola Nordmann drink? In this respect, he is pretty much

98. While all the reindeer in northern
Norway are domesticated animals,
large herds of wild reindeer still roam
highland areas in the south, as here in
the Rondane mountain massif.
(R. Frislid/NN)

98

*99. In the dusk of a spring evening,
elk graze on the lush vegetation beside
lakes and streams.* (Pål Hermansen/
Samfoto/NN) ▷

100. Long, shallow boats are used for
navigating the big rivers in Finnmark.
Today they are fitted with outboard
motors, but in many places it is still
necessary to pole along, as in the old
days. (Hans Hvide Bang/Samfoto)

101. An old boat-house stands sentry
against the sea at Bremangerlandet in
western Norway. The fine sandy
beaches here would be crowded
were the climate a little warmer.
(R. Frislid/NN)

102

102. The area of the community of Alta (Finmark county) is one of the richest in Europe in prehistoric rock carvings. Many of these, which number 1,600–1,700, depict animals and hunting scenes. The carvings may be up to 6,000 years old. (R. Frislid/NN)

103. The elk thrives in all wooded areas, from north to south, and from the lowlands to the mountain forests. (Pål Hermansen/Samfoto/NN)

104. Each spring the Reindeer Såmis move their animals to the islands off the coast of Finnmark. During this trek, many of the reindeer-owners spend the nights in their traditional tents, pitched in a circle around a blazing fire. (Hand Hvide Bang/Samfoto/NN) ▷

a creature of habit: it is not permitted to advertise alcohol to introduce new brands, just as tobacco advertising is forbidden. (A law passed in 1988 also restricts smoking at work or in public places.) However, the grapevine works in such a way that fashions in drinking change from time to time. His increased affluence has also given him a more refined palate: it is no longer the one standard 'red' that is served at a big dinner.

Norwegians do not really drink very much — at least officially. According to 1985 statistics, France had a consumption of 13.3 litres of spirits per habitant, while Norway was right at the bottom of the league with 4.2 litres. For instance, Kari and Ola drank only 48 litres of beer each in 1985 (as against 172 litres of milk!), while West Germans drank 146 litres, East Germans 142, Czechs 131, and the Danes 121 litres of beer. And beer does have a longstanding tradition in Norway. The communal bowl of ale was found in all homes. Brewing was ritual and mystical. The ingredients were barley malt, juniper and hops, and sometimes grated potatoes. When the yeast was added, the Norwegian was supposed to start yelling — to make the beer stronger. But while it was fermenting, one had to be careful not to stamp one's feet, bang doors or talk in a loud voice, as this could stop the process.

Many still brew their own beer for Christmas and other occasions, yet home brewing generally is on the decline: most people get their supply at the supermarket. Norwegian beer does not have the same worldwide fame as Danish Tuborg or Carlsberg. However, the breweries of Schou, Frydenlund and Ringnes in Oslo, Hansa in Bergen, and Mack in Tromsø have maintained the traditions of the southern European brewers who once came to teach us how to make beer. Rather successfully in fact: at an exclusive contest in Belgium in 1987, the small Nordland Brewery from Bodø was proclaimed the best in the world.

Norwegians are modest wine drinkers, downing a mere five litres on average in 1986, while the Portuguese drank 87 and the French 80. The Wine Monopoly stocks a wide range of good wines from most producer countries. A little wine is also produced in Norway, mostly from locally-grown fruit such as rhubarb, cherries, redcurrants. Home production is increasingly popular, mainly using wine kits from the wine producers. For some strange reason there is no law against this.

The Russians have their vodka, the Dutch their Genever, and the Norwegians their *akevitt, aqua vitae*, Latin for 'water of life'. Aquavit is a spiced liquor, made from the potato — the grape of the north — according to ancient and secret recipes that include cumin, fennel, coriander, bitter-orange peel, aniseed, and the essence of 50 other herbs and spices. It has to be stored in an oak cask that has previously contained sherry. If the aquavit is to be really good it has to travel at least two or three months on a Wilh. Wilhelmsen ship that crosses the Equator. For many years the passage was to Australia, but now the route has been changed. However, the effect is the same: the motion and the variations in temperature make the aquavit extra mature.

It is estimated that home distilling increased from 1.2 litres in 1956 to 4.4 litres in 1986, that is, to more than one litre per Norwegian.

There were 6,800 sentences for drunken driving in 1985 (3.9 for every 1,000 cars) and 32,284 arrests for drunken behaviour. We are now talking mainly about Ola Nordmann — only 2,500 of those arrested were women. Even if Ola Nordmann drinks the least in Europe, he drinks the fastest! The Saturday-night binge is a well-known national phenomenon. Considering the price of drink in Norway, cirrhosis of the liver is quite a status symbol.

105. Norway is a mountainous land, two thirds of it lying above or north of the timber line. In Jotunheimen, the central mountain massif in southern Norway, many peaks rise well above 2,000 metres (6,000 feet). (R. Frislid/NN)

FARMING AND FISHING

CHAPTER EIGHT is about the Norwegian farmer who tills his land in the short summer and is paid the same as a factory worker, and the Norwegian fisherman who braves the cruel sea.

The Norwegian farmer, who is he?

Is he the splendid, proud, silent man, the loner, the *Übermensch* as we know him from novelist Trygve Gulbranssen's trilogy of the 1930s, *Beyond Sing the Woods*, a work translated into 30 languages and filmed several times?

Or is he like Isak Sellanraa, in Knut Hamsun's *Growth of the Soil*, who breaks the ground with the sweat of his brow, and ends up so wealthy he can go out into the pasture and count his horse!

Foreigners have made various attempts to describe him through the centuries. Our French travelling companion, Jacques de la Tocnaye, met him on his journey in 1799 after coming back over the mountains to the eastern part of the country:

"The people on this side of the mountains seem to belong to another category altogether, and this becomes increasingly obvious the further east you travel. They are as friendly and generous as the people of Bergen are quarrelsome and greedy. Further inland you find wealthier, in fact, some very wealthy farmers, some of whom behave in a highly polished manner. These people do not deserve to be called peasants, for in other countries they would be considered gentlemen."

About a century later in their classic travelogue *Three in Norway — by Two of Them*, J.A. Lees and W.J. Clutterbuck describe the natives as "immeasurably slow. We have studied these people and have come to the conclusion that nothing we do can make them increase their pace, while on the contrary it takes very little to make them slow down. When it comes to old people, it is indeed a rarity to see them move at all. Norwegian boys are so lively and full of explosive energy that they are never satisfied unless they are in at least three places at once. But when they attain the age of fifteen and their parents let them eat their fill, their restlessness completely disappears and gives way to a kind of apathetic paralysis." The Englishmen had collected these observations from the mountain villages around Jotunheimen.

After yet another century, the general secretary of the Farmers' Union, Hans Haga, asserted in 1986: "Our farmers are tradition-bound and conservative, and so proud of their roots that innovation is difficult for them."

It is quite clear that the farm itself and the consciousness of ancient traditions have meant a great deal in this country, where agriculture has been carried on for at least 6,000 years, and where there have been farms for perhaps 2,500 years. Burial grounds on the old farms tell us about these worthy freeholders and their authoritative wives. The deep ruts made by horses' hooves from farm to farm show the close contact between the ancient homesteads, and the fortified villages of the Iron Age point to the farmers' need to protect themselves against intruders. The more cut-off the mountain village or the valley, the stronger the family pride. It was no coincidence that the Norwegian Nazis' romantic cult of old rural traditions gained most adherents in isolated areas such as Valle in Setesdal, Finsland in Vest-Agder, Tolga, Dovre and other mountain villages in east Norway.

Not much of the country bumpkin is left in the modern Norwegian farmer. He is young, dynamic and well-educated. He wears a suit, carries a briefcase, and is an expert on battery hens, bacon factories, greenhouses, accountancy and pesticides! According to the Conservative paper *Aftenposten*, he is the richest farmer in the world. This is partly due to the fact that he has been good at organizing himself. There are two main unions for farmers, one for the big and one for the small: the Farmers' Union and the Farmer and Smallholders' Union. There is also a powerful Forestry Union and co-operatives for everything from fertilizers to milk production. They even have one of the greatest youth organizations in the country, 4H, which stands for a clear Head, a warm Heart, clever Hands and good Health. It has 25,000 members — and there are only 100,000 farmers in Norway.

No-one can claim that a country so far north, with such meagre soil and so short a summer, is ideal for agriculture. But when Ola Nordmann was hungry during the German occupation in the Second World War, he realized the importance of being self-sufficient in food. Politicians therefore decided, when faced with the task of building Norway up again after the war, that agriculture should get the same opportunities as other areas of production. In 1975 it was even established by law that agricultural workers were to have the same wages as industrial workers, and farmers' incomes were heavily boosted by state subsidies. In 1987, however, the Labour Party discovered that the subsidies had not had the desired effect. On the contrary, they had made the rich farmers in the fertile eastern areas even richer, while smallholders, particularly farmers in outlying districts, had not reaped the same benefit from the subsidies. While the State had favoured the large farms, leading to a certain extent to surplus production, each year 3,000 small farms were being abandoned. This could hardly be said to counteract the flight from the countryside and did lead to some shift in priorities.

Norway is not alone in supporting agriculture. In 1987, the 24 OECD countries used the equivalent of 1,000 billion kroner to help farmers, and the cost to EEC countries of storing the surplus production alone amounted to more than the total agricultural subsidies of Norway. The other OECD countries try desperately to reduce outlays for farm support, despite massive protests from farmers. In Norway the response to the retrenchment of 1987 was the biggest farmers' demonstration ever held. From hill farms, plains, valleys and coastal areas some 10,000 poured into the capital and marched to Youngstorvet, the traditional battlesite of the Labour movement. Their slogans were: 'Keep your village alive!', 'If the farmer goes, the country dies!', 'Stop witch-hunting farmers!' They were tired, they said, of being ostracized and described as parasites.

When pointing out the differences between farmers in 1799, Jacques de la Tocnaye said he thought the inland farmers were easier to get on with than the 'fish-eaters' of the coast: "Up here in the mountain valleys, where the warmth of the sun is reflected from the hills, the grain ripens more quickly than by the coast, and it follows that people are much more content. Nonetheless, most people live by the coast, where they drag out their days, imagining that they would die of grief if they could not look out to sea."

The crofter in Finnmark has as little in common with the rich farmer of the east as does the smallholder on the west coast who has for generations carried the hay on his back from outyling patches of pasture-land. In 1985 the net income of each farm in the eastern areas was 228,200 kroner, compared with 245,300 in Jæren and 143,600 in north Norway. In fact, the west coast farmer has now rationalized and taken his cow off the farm, turning to strawberry production and salmon farming instead!

The annual general meeting of the local dairy used to be the place where you could see the Norwegian small farmer in his element. In a convival atmosphere that had a whiff of the barnyard, the farmers would meet in the school or chapel to drink coffee and discuss milk prices. When it came to the price of milk, the Norwegian farmer was on sure ground, yet he had to argue against well-spoken dairy specialists who had been to agricultural college. But the farmers had to watch the small homesteads disappear and a milk factory take over. They had to capitulate to rationalization experts who promised ten øre more per litre if only they could bring about a merger with the dairy in the next village, which again could be amalgamated with the county dairy, which could be taken over by the district dairy. Now there are only 19 dairy companies left, and the Norwegian Milk Board won't give up until the whole thing is one vast company.

Farms are also decreasing in number, but getting larger and more efficient: in 1939 there were 215,000, by 1985 only 105,000. Today's farm averages 23 acres with 22 head of cattle and 66 sheep, as against seven and 17 respectively a generation ago. Though 3,000 farms disappear every year, the total acreage has been stable in recent years as farms have been taken over by other farms, or because the surviving farmers rent any spare land.

If we include Svalbard, we have a total area of 100 million acres, of which only 9.5 million are farmed and 66 million consist of workable forestry land. Half the farmed area is pastureland or used for grazing, though one third of the land provides 30 per cent of the grain eaten in Norway. The politicians say we must grow more food, and that the aim is to be self-sufficient in meat, potatoes and storable vegetables. Norwegian produce, including fish and meat, makes up 53 per cent of the total calory intake. The rest has to be imported.

Forestry has also undergone a drastic rationalization process since the war. The horse and sleigh have been replaced by the tractor on the forest road, and the local sawmill is a thing of the past. The largest company for the conversion of wood products is Norwegian Forestry Industries, started in 1966 by the organization of forestry owners and 13,000 shareholders. Today the company has a turnover of 3 billion kroner, mainly in the field of newsprint. Some nine million cubic metres (11.8 cubic yards) of timber, mostly coniferous, were felled annually in Norway in the 1980s. Half of this went to sawmills and wood products, the rest for wood pulp and chemical pulp. Nothing is as friendly and evocative of home comfort as chimney smoke on a still, frosty morning, but most people today heat their houses by oil or electricity. Of all the nine million cubic metres of timber, only 300,000 are used for firewood.

When autumn comes, primitive instincts are awakened in Ola Nordmann, and it is no longer safe to go out into the countryside! When the men gather at first light with their guns and red caps, it becomes clear that the elk hunt must be the Norwegian tradition closest to the ancient heathen rituals of the hunting tribe. In some places the school gives the children a day off so that the eldest sons can be in on the sacrificial killing from a tender age. In 1985, 25,000 elks were brought down by 32,000 hunters. Many also hit other things, such as tractors and horses. Though the statistics keep quiet about this, the press does not. The local papers give detailed reports on the hunting with the names of the good marksmen and the weight of the dead animal, thereby confirming the importance of the hunt as a tradition.

Big-game hunting in Norway brought in five million kilos (4,910 tons) of meat in 1985, while small-game or general hunting brought in one million kilos. The total volume of meat from livestock breeding comes to 180 million kilos (176,000 tons), which means that game accounts for 3.5 per cent of Norway's total meat consumption. Notwithstanding all this hunting, it is a fact that the numbers of elk, reindeer and deer have increased tenfold since the war.

The strange thing is that while rural areas are being depopulated in Norway, there are more and more hunters. In the decade up to 1985, the number rose from 120,000 to 185,000, 4,000 of whom were women. Some relate this to increased affluence, as more people can afford to go hunting. Grouse shooting has become a mass sport: 80,000 people go out every year, and in 1985 they bagged 700,000 grouse and ptarmigan. As the sport becomes more popular, the hunter runs the risk of no longer being the great hero he was to the ancient tribes. In fact, he may well be looked upon as a despoiler of the countryside and a status-seeker.

There are foxes, bears, wolves and wolverines in the woods, though you may not meet them when out walking. A hundred years ago bears were to be found in forests all over Norway, and most villages could boast of a hunter who had shot a prestigious total, but by 1965 there were perhaps less than 50 left. At the beginning of the 1970s bears,

Kitchen utensils from the Oseberg ship. Viking Age.

wolves and wolverines became protected species, and the numbers of bears and wolverines have increased accordingly. Today there are problably 250 bears and 200 wolverines. Most of the former are in the wooded areas between Sweden and Norway, though the occasional one is sighted in every county except Vestfold. Wolverines are usually to be found where there are reindeer, but they rove over the whole country. There is no danger now of either of these species becoming extinct.

Wolves are a rarer breed. After the war they were to be found in the north, while the south was reckoned to be wolf-free. Lately the wolf has had to give way to the motorized ski-scooter in the north, though a pack of about 30 has grown up in the forests of the south between Glåmdalen and Värmland in Sweden. In Finland there is a very much larger pack of about 200 animals.

Not all farmers love these predators, which caused damage and loss of livestock worth about 7 million kroner in 1986. The wolverine is the worst sinner, killing 200 reindeer and 2,000 sheep a year. The bear will also attack sheep, and then the farmer gets his gun and goes out with a special licence from the Royal Ministry of Agriculture.

From now on wildlife should be even better protected. Norway has signed the Council of Europe's convention aimed at safeguarding flora and fauna, and has worked out a comprehensive plan for the protection of bears, wolverines and wolves. Six special areas have been designated covering one third of the country, where animals can roam in safety. So now it's up to them to stick to the regulations!

Fishing, along with hunting, is the most ancient occupation in Norway. Since being washed ashore under the edge of the ice some 10,000 years ago with fish hook and harpoon of bone and antler in his hide boat, the fisherman here has become used to fending for himself in the struggle against wind and weather and sea — the mysterious ocean that hides so much and where every creature is part of a chain: the whale and the seal linked to the large fish, the large fish to the smaller, the small fish to animal plankton, and animal plankton to plant plankton . . .

He went to the nearest coast and to the most distant waters for his catch, and as time went by the number of fishermen grew. The hide boat and bone tackle were replaced by sail and steam, harpoon guns and depth charges. In the 1880s up to 33,000 men took part in the legendary cod fishing off the Lofoten Islands. In the 1930s, 10,000 Norwegians were working on the other side of the globe, in the floating whale factories of the Antarctic.

New kinds of animals came, old kinds of fish disappeared, and the Norwegian fisherman did not always display the greatest wisdom. He was still learning the hard way as recently as 1987, when he found his nets full of seals. There had been seals in Eastern Finnmark for many years, but now the whole northern part of Norway was suddenly invaded by these creatures that ate the cod and ruined equipment for the Lofoten fishermen.

There are an estimated four million Greenland seals in the world, half of them in Newfoundland, the rest on the East Ice of the Barents Sea and the West Ice off Greenland. In the winter of 1986–87, around half a million turned up on the Norwegian coast, and 50,000 of them were caught in the fishing nets and filled up one refrigerator plant after another — in place of the fish that were nowhere to be seen! It was a total catastrophe. Many of the seals had fatty tissue of a mere 20 millimetres (less than an inch), which is the minimum they need not to freeze to eath. Since each seal eats about five kilos (11 lbs) of fish a day, this vast number consumed about 75,000 tons a month — more than the whole Lofoten season's catch. These seals were ravenously hungry.

The seal was not the only one to go hungry. Leif and Trond Fredriksen, fishermen from Svolvær, the largest town in Lofoten, were interviewed by *Dagbladet* in 1987, six weeks into the Lofoten fishing season. After yet another day with a 'black sea', this is what father and son had to say:

"We have no explanation for what is happening. It is frightening. Many fishermen are really scared. We just don't know what to do with ourselves. What little cod we have caught is without liver or roe, and practically without guts. It is black inside and emaciated. On the Finnmark coast some of the fish we caught had their snouts worn down from eating seaweed, for want of anything better. We have had bad times in Lofoten before, but this is different. This is serious. Today we caught not one fish in 35 nets..."

At the same time a deathly silence fell over the bird rocks on Bjørnøya (Bear Island) in the Barents Sea. In 1986 there were 400,000 common guillemots nesting there. The following year only one tenth were left. The decrease had long been noticeable in Troms and West Finnmark. The sea birds were so short of food, so desperate, that at least 100,000 guillemots drowned in the cod fishing nets off Outer Troms.

How could this happen? What were the reasons for this seal invasion, for the starvation, the dead birds, and the catastrophe which brought nature to such a cruel imbalance and resulted in the government paying compensation to fishermen? There was a heated discussion about this for some months. Most people were of the opinion that the Barents Sea had simply been fished out. The food chain here consists of plankton, herring, capelin, cod, haddock, saithe, whale and seal, with man straddling the pyramid. Oceanographers had warned against drawing too heavily on the capelin, the small fish that is the food of both the cod and the seal, yet the authorities allowed for a large quota. The result was that the capelin population sank from 2.6 million tons to less than 100,000 tons in the years 1984 to 1987, while the cod population decreased in direct proportion. Then large fishing trawls swept the Barents Sea clean of capelin. The larder was bare. The chain had been broken. Hence the starving cod and the wandering seal.

"It is gross overfishing. It is almost unbelievable that the authorities allowed the trawling fleet to wipe out the capelin. It is one of the most direct causes of the ecological catastrophe we can see approaching. But it seems as if it is the authorities that understand the least," said the Fredriksens, two generations of fishermen from Svolvær.

They are two of Norway's 30,000 professional fishermen. Thirty years ago there were twice as many. Half the fishermen are from the north of Norway, but only two out of three have fishing as a full-time occupation.

As one can see, the catch varies a good deal, according to the whims of the authorities and Mother Nature. Normally Norwegian fishermen haul 2.5 million tons of fish yearly out of the sea. That means that Norway, with one thousandth of the world population, has three to four per cent of the world's fishing. Only Japan, the Soviet Union, China, the U.S.A. and Chile fish more than Norway. About one third of the total catch consists of capelin, while cod, saithe and herring make up about one tenth each. Shrimp fishing produces just under 100,000 tons. We export 90 per cent of the fish, mainly to EC countries, the U.S.A. and

Japan. This brings in almost nine billion kroner, and represents 10 per cent of our total exports apart from ships and petroleum. Only about five per cent of the fish is distributed fresh; 20 per cent is frozen, and about 60 per cent is used in manufacturing oil, fishmeal and other products.

The average Norwegian eats 38 kilos (83.6 pounds) of fish a year, less than a third in its fresh form. This includes the popular mackerel in tomato sauce, and the favourite Norwegian dishes – incomprehensible to all foreigners – fishballs and fishpudding!

The catch is mostly from the Norwegian coastal zone and outside the 200-mile limit from the Svalbard area and near Jan Mayen. Less than 15 per cent is fished in other countries' zones.

There are approximately 25,000 fishing boats, two-thirds of them open and used only during a short part of the year for coastal fishing for cod and sprat, herring, lobster and crab. It is the large boats that make the profits.

The industry is exceedingly well regulated. Norway was the first country in the world to set up a separate Fisheries Ministry, in 1946, and has its own state bank for fishermen. The 20,000-member-strong Norwegian Fishermen's Association can demand state subsidies if the catch is not good enough, a practice that seems to have become permanent.

In the inter-war years the price of fish varied from day to day and from village to village. There are no fish auctions in Norway as in other countries. In many fishing villages there was only one buyer and he set the price. The Depression in the 30s was hard on fishermen, but in 1936 they were guaranteed a minimum price for fish that was to be salted or dried, and in 1938 they acquired their 'constitution', the Raw Fish Act, which enabled them to sell the fish through their own joint companies. They now sell through Norway's Raw Fish Association, which has its establishments along the entire coastline from Finnmark to Nordmøre, as well as 13 other sales companies.

Today there are about 700 centres of the fish industry in Norway, employing around 16,000 people. Drying and salting of fish is carried out along large stretches of the coast, much as in the days when the Italian nobleman and merchant Pietro Querini landed on the windblown island of Røst in Lofoten in 1431. He was on his way from Crete to Flanders with a cargo of wine, but seems to have navigated as erratically as the Vikings who found themselves in America. He was, however, so enthusiastic about the Norwegian stockfish that he informed the Pope about it, and thus opened up a unique new market for the Norwegians.

'Stockfish – Viking food with a long tradition!' advertise the Norwegian fish exporters, and underline the differences between salted fish, klipfish and stockfish. Salted fish is decapitated, gutted and skinned, has its backbone removed, and is laid in brine for a minimum of three weeks before it can be sold, either whole or in fillets. The saltfish is used as the raw material for the klipfish, which is fish cleaned, salted and dried. In former years it was dried in the open on the cliff (klippe), hence the name. Today the drying takes place in a special warm-air unit. The first klipfish was dried at the time when Columbus went to America. In the seventeenth century it became an important Norwegian export. Today bacalao is part of the diet in many Catholic countries, especially Portugal, Brazil and Italy. Stockfish is unsalted fish dried in the open solely by wind and sun. This is what one sees hanging on the drying racks in Norwegian fishing villages.

108

108. Long distances and difficult weather conditions for boats and motor vehicles make the airplane invaluable, especially in northern Norway. This is the airfield at Båtsfjord, Finnmark. (Husmo-Foto)

109. Out to the oil field:
a drilling rig being towed out of
Oslo – fjord. (Hans Hvide Bang/
Samfoto/NN) ▷

110. Oil drilling rig at Gansfjorden,
Stavanger. Platforms for deep-sea
drilling have become a new speciality
of the shipbuilding industry. (Husmo-
Foto) ▷ ▷

111

112

111. The waterway of canals, locks and sluices in Telemark county was completed in 1892. It helps the old 'Victoria' to lift her load of tourists up to Lake Bandak in the heart of Telemark, 100 kilometres (60 miles) from the starting point at the city of Skien, and some 70 metres (230 feet) above sea level. (R. Frislid/NN)

112. Although new bridges are being built all the time, car ferries still play a decisive role in maintaining communications in western Norway, as here at Utne in the Hardanger district. (M. Løberg/Samfoto)

113. Thanks to the helicopter, the transportation of building materials to construction sites in remote places no longer presents a problem. (Husma-Foto)

114. At Kylling in Romsdalen trains roll across this impressive stone bridge high above the famous salmon river of Rauma. The bridge dates from 1924. (Mittet)

115. Small landing strips unite the country: Norway today has some 50 airfields regularly served by commercial flights. (Per-Anders Rosenkvist/Samfoto)

116

116. More and more women are to be found in jobs traditionally held by men. This applies even on the oil rigs in the North Sea. (Betten Fosse/ Samfoto)

117. Heavily loaded with food for thought, this floating library, the 'book boat', finds its way to distant settlements and isolated communities in western Norway. (Helge Sunde) ▷

Despite regulations and good organization, some fishermen are more equal than others, and this difference is not likely to diminish in the future. Today there are nine factory ships in the Norwegian fishing fleet, but in the next few years we can reckon on a large number of saltfish and freezer trawlers with refrigeration plants being converted into fish factories. This will be beneficial to the shipowners of Møre, but will weaken the fishermen of the north — or so they fear.

The fishing smack owner Stein Hansen told *Dagbladet* how this aspect of the North-South conflict hits the individual, as in Øyhellsundet in Lofoten, where experts urged that the herring be protected, but the authorities let the 'large-scale' fishermen get them.

''It's almost like war,'' said Stein Hansen from Gratangen, come all the way from his home village to fish his legal quota. ''We small fishermen are chased away, while these huge trawlers pump up everything they come across. Soon there will be no more herring here, mark my words!''

The herring is an unreliable visitor! No one knows when he's coming, no one knows when he's going. But when he does turn up, he creates quite a stir! The herring appears on the Scandinavian coast in periodical large waves of migration. The last great wave of winter herring came to Norway in the 1950s, when 2,800 vessels and 25,000 men were employed in fishing for the herring. The largest shoals came to the west coast, but herring oil factories were to be found right up into the Oslo fjord, 'smelling of money'. In one single year, 1956, 1.7 million tons were caught. Fantastic!

And then there was all that came in its wake. There was a boom in fish barrels, and in small sawmills all round the coast people were busy making barrel staves. Others worked day and night to pack the fish into the barrels so that it lay there in layers, properly gutted, belly up, in such strong brine that a potato with a nail in it could stay afloat. That was how it should be!

But people are greedy, and well-equipped. In modern times fishermen have gone out to meet the herring on the banks with drift nets and seines. By the end of the 60s all the herring had been fished, and many small towns on the west coast found themselves in difficulties. The herring was totally protected for some years, and more than half the herring oil factories closed down. However, the stock is increasing again according to old hands who had large catches of herring in the North Sea in 1987.

Herring was the poor man's food. Salmon, on the other hand, is the rich man's food! Ola Nordmann's aim is to turn the salmon into a domestic animal. In the 1960s he began in a small way to breed salmon commercially. One fish farm after another appeared in Norwegian fjords and creeks, and salmon-breeding was hailed as the new economic wonder. The new 'coastal aristocracy' grew rich. In 1986, 40,000 tons of salmon worth around two billion kroner were exported to 20 countries; 99 per cent of the fish had been bred commercially. There were up to 700 hatcheries, 5,000 people were directly employed in fish farming, and 2,000 more were queueing up to start sea farms. Many Norwegians had also become involved in fish farms abroad.

But it is not easy to tame the salmon. *Salmo salmar* is used to having the whole Atlantic around him, and when confined in a small space, he suffers from stress, cold water vibriosis, and lice, ending up having to be cured with large doses of antibiotics and nerve gas. New dangers are

118. Tranøy lighthouse in Hamarøy (Nordland county) is one of nearly 100 manned lighthouses along the coast. On clear summer nights in northern Norway, the lighthouses are not lit. (R. Frislid/ NN)

always lurking. During the frightening environmental catastrophe of 1988, when the Skagerrak was invaded by poisonous algae that killed all fish, the fish farmers had to flee further north with their hatcheries. Fish farmers now put their trust in a vaccine against cold water vibriosis or 'Hitra disease', as it is called in Norway, and they are planning to breed other kinds of fish such as halibut and turbot, catfish and plaice.

The fishmonger in the famous Bergen fish market has taken up the challenge and now puts up a large notice advertising 'Wild salmon'!

And still we have the wild cod. From time immemorial cod have swum to the coast by the millions to spawn, from Lopphavet to Trøndelag, but in particular on the north side of Vestfjorden, from Lødingen to Røst, giving cause for the adventure that is the richest in tradition and lore: the Lofoten fishery.

There have been mass migrations to the Lofoten fishery, there have been fabulous catches, and there have been black years.

"They came from the west country. From Trøndelag, Nordland Troms and Finmark they came. There were fishermen, cooks, rookies, baitsmen, menders of nets as well as of bicycles, peddlers, Jews and jewellers, fire-and-brimstone preachers, and conjurors. Each had his own idea of Lofoten and what he could get there. They were after fish that would give them the kind of money they had never had before. This was in the order of things, whether they made a living from pulling an oar or selling pastries and cheap watches to the fishermen." The north Norwegian folklorist and author Frank A. Jenssen gives us this description in his colourful book on the Lofoten fishery.

In 1895 the greatest number of fishermen ever seen in Lofoten, 32,600 in all, brought in 125,000 tons of spawning cod. The peak was in 1947, when 20,500 men caught 146,000 tons. In the 1980s only about 4,000 people were taking advantage of the Lofoten fishing season, and the catch was around 50,000 tons. When the great seal invasion came in 1987, the results were so poor that buyers had to get in fish from far away in order to cover the Italian market.

The organization of the Lofoten fishery goes back a long way. In the Viking period there were laws to ensure that the chieftains got their share of the catch. Most of the dried fish that was brought into Bergen a thousand years ago came from Lofoten. At the beginning of the eighteenth century all the fishing was done with a hand-held line, which Norwegian fishermen today call the *juksa*. Then, a few decades later, came the long line and the use of nets, so the authorities had to divide up the fishing grounds.

The traditional vessel was the *fembøring*, an open boat with five pairs of oars, or the *attring* with four pairs or eight oars, both of them square-rigged and narrow, like a Viking ship. In 1905 the motor boat started to take over. Then, after the Second World War, came radar, the echo sounder, sonar, all excellent means of plotting the whereabouts of the fish, and these were followed by the hydraulic winch to hoist the catch on board, and satellite-linked navigation that can help steer the boat to within yards of the shoal.

Today it is the fishermen themselves who determine how the sea is to be divided up, and the fish is caught with hand-held lines, long lines, nets, and trawls. Out on the fishing grounds there is a difference between the rich and the poor, between those who hold a single line in their hands and those with large nets.

In his book, Jenssen describes them all, and everything in connecion with the Lofoten fishery: its drinking traditions and the women who t one time in the last century made an immoral living. Above all he describes today's participants — from the fisherman with his hand-held ine and jig with red woollen thread or rubber worm who growls that trawling is dirty fishing', to the fishery magnate Arne W. Johansen, who wns the whole of Stamsund and lives in a palace by north Norwegian tandards. Also included are the tongue cutters, that little closed shop of children between the ages of eight and sixteen who cut out the cods' ongues in accordance with unwritten medieval laws. In his book, there s the lifeboat that comes to the rescue of vessels with nets in their propellors. There is the boiler that in an infernal atmosphere heats up od liver oil to 970°C in seven minutes. He presents the Fisherman's Retreat that serves waffles and the Word of God, the fishery protection nspectors who have police authority in matters concerning the fishing grounds, the women who toil in the bait rooms and on board. He tells us bout the feast that follows the first catch of spawning cod, with a special oup called *mølje,* served with roe, liver, stomach, blood, beer and aquavit.

He describes the stockfish taster, Lofoten's counterpart of the connoisseur wine taster, who has held an official position since 1716, after Querini had told His Holiness about the stockfish of Røst. The taster ensures that all fish sent to Rome or other places are of top quality. He has to rely on his nose, his eyes and his tastebuds to determine to which of the 26 classes each fish belongs. There is a true Italian ring to the names of the categories: *Vestre Piccolo, Vestre Piccolo Piccolo, Vestre*

Illustration (by the authors) to 'Three in Norway by Two of Them', by J.A. Lees and W.J. Clutterbuck, first published in 1882, reprinted by Aschehoug in 1988.

Demi Magro, Anakona Vestre, Grand Premier — and *Ragno*, the jewel of them all, the spawning cod with golden belly and translucent sides.

There is still cod to be had in the Barents Sea, say the experts; there is in fact a great deal of cod, if only it gets enough capelin to feed on and escapes yet another invasion of seals. But these prophecies are not always matched by the experience of the fishermen.

Because of the seal disaster of 1987, many Norwegians wanted to step up sealhunting, which had all but come to a halt. In the 1970s Norwegians caught 300,000 seals a year in the East Ice and West Ice. In 1987 only five or six state-subsidized ships went off to kill some 10,000 animals — a decrease due to international protests and threats of boycott because of the way seal cubs were culled: hunters battered the baby seals to death using a club on their little skulls.

But what happened to the Norwegian whaler? He too is giving up. Whaling has been carried on since prehistoric times. Basques caught whales in the Bay of Biscay in the ninth century, the English and Dutch off Svalbard in the seventeenth, and in the eighteenth, the Americans started their whaling activities. Norwegians have hunted for whales for as long as they have lived in Norway.

In the old days whale fishing meant hurling a hand harpoon from a rowing boat after small whales that, when captured, would float on their own blubber. It was not until 1868, when the Norwegian whaler Svend Foyn invented the harpoon gun and developed the steam-driven whaling ship, that whaling really took off. It increased so dramatically that from 1904 the whale had to be protected along the Norwegian coast.

After this the Norwegians threw themselves into a merciless hunt for whales in the Antarctic, with the result that the creature was near extinction by the 1960s, though it must be said that the Norwegians were not the only ones to blame. Before 1912 there were seven whaling stations on South Georgia, four of them Norwegian. Thousands upon thousands of whalers from the towns in Vestfold went south. At the beginning of the 1930s there were 41 Norwegian whaling factories and six shore stations in the South Atlantic. In the middle of the 1930s as many as 17,000 whales were harpooned by Norwegians in the Antarctic, and the gigantic mammals, weighing up to 150 tons, were pumped full of air and towed to the floating whale factories. At times Norway produced 80 per cent of the world's whale oil.

Large whales were still being hunted after the Second World War, but by 1960 there were not many left. The blue whale became a protected species in 1963, the baleen whale in 1964, and the fin whale in the southern hemisphere in 1977. Norway closed its last whaling station in the Antarctic in 1968.

Since the 1920s Norway has been catching minke whale commercially, with a peak catch of 4,000 whales a year. In the 1980s this activity was drastically reduced, and in 1987, 53 boats, mainly from Nordland, were licensed to catch 375 whales.

When Prime Minister Gro Harlem Brundtland presented the United Nations environmental report *Our Common Future* in London in 1987, the Greenpeace organization asked her to put her own house in order and stop that year's massacre of whales, the 'barbaric environmental vandalism' that is anathema to the international community. And she promised. She declared that all commercial Norwegian whaling was to cease after the 1987 season, in accordance with the statutes of the International Whaling Commission, and under pressure from the U.S.A.

SEAMEN AND SHIPPING

CHAPTER NINE is the story of the Norwegian seaman who sailed Norway from poverty to riches, and the shipowners who kicked him out when he became too expensive.

No-one is the subject of so much touching emotion as the rookie, the young boy who packed his bags, waved farewell to his mother, dried a tear, and left his small village in the mountains or by the coast. When he returned six months later he was a fully-fledged sailor, the hero of his peer group, having had his initiation in the storms of Biscay and the brothels of Hamburg.

For over a century women have been sitting in the Seaman's Missions knitting garments for those brave unknown boys away at sea, gifts that have been collected and handed out by the Norwegian Seaman's Church when the ship reached harbour.

It is hardly surprising that Ola Nordmann feels the sea in his bones considering that his long country has 2,650 kilometres (1,645 miles) of coastline following the most direct route from the Swedish to the Russian border. If you take in every bay and creek and stretch that distance out, you will have travelled 21,347 kilometres (13,256 miles), or almost half way round the world.

Norwegian children have always been taught that their country has the world's greatest tonnage of shipping in proportion to the population. We have all been brought up on pictures of ships in foreign ports, in Houston and Durban, San Francisco and Hong Kong. For years the newspapers gave exact positions of all Norwegian ships around the world, so that mother and father could send their letters to the nearest seaman's church.

Yet Norwegian shipping has had its ups and downs.

The first setback came in the thirteenth century when Viking ships were unable to compete with the beamier, decked Hanseatic trading vessels. In the sixteenth century the Dutch came in search of timber, and later that century Norwegian shipping picked up again. By the nineteenth century shipping provided a good revenue for the country.

The last century was the age of sail. Sailing ships were anchored so close together in the Norwegian harbours that small boys could run dry-footed across them. The tonnage increased from 100,000 in 1830 to 1.4 millions in 1890. Today Norway has only three square-rigged tall ships left as a reminder of those days. Then came ships driven by steam and engines, there were two world wars, and in the last war the whole merchant fleet was put at the service of the Allies.

The world fleet increased from 80 million registered tons in 1948 to 290 million in 1973, and at that time Norway with her one thousandth of the world population had 10 per cent of the world tonnage. In the 1970s each Norwegian had on average 7,000 tons, each Briton 600, each Japanese 375, and each American 70 tons.

Then came the big shock. In 1973 oil prices rose, trade generally was on the way down, and there were far too many tankers in the world! One ship after another was laid up. At the beginning of the 80s around 50 giant tankers were in their moorings − 40 per cent of the Norwegian tanker fleet.

The Norwegian shipowners then agreed among themselves that their own seamen had become too expensive, making Norway uncompetitive on the world market. They found that it would be cheaper to bring in people from the Third World who would be willing to sign on for a fraction of a Norwegian's pay. By this means they could save 4 million kroner per ship per year, or 1.2 billion for the whole fleet.

But then the ships could no longer sail under the Norwegian flag so they would have to fly a so-called 'flag of convenience', from Liberia, Panama, Bahamas or some other tax haven. Norwegian seamen have always despised ships registered under such flags. On board these vessels, the men have been treated indifferently, with none of the rights Norwegian seamen have fought for concerning pay, conditions and safety regulations. Sometimes the people taken on board were made to sign two contracts, one that could be shown to ITF, the International Transport Workers Federation, and one that laid down their real conditions.

But Norwegian shipowners had made up their minds to register abroad. In the mid-80s the Conservative government softened the restrictions on this, and by 1987, 455 Norwegian-owned vessels of 14.57 million tons deadweight were sailing under flags of convenience, while only 512, amounting to 9.76 million tons, were registered at home. The largest shipping lines applied for permission to register abroad, including the giant Bergesen line, whose tonnage equalled one third of the remaining Norwegian fleet. Not even our large cruise ships were spared, ships that for years had sailed from Miami with the Norwegian flag rippling in the wind. This was even the fate of Norway's flagship, the S/S *Norway*, formerly the French liner *France*.

By the beginning of 1987 Norway had for the first time dropped out

Horce-racing on ice. Illustration to Olaus Magnus: 'History of the Nordic Peoples', Rome 1555.

f the list of the ten most important shipping nations in the world. A decade before she had been listed fourth. Registration abroad coincided with a total collapse of the oil-rig and supply-ship market. Thousands of seamen were laid off and made redundant.

The Norwegian sailor was in danger of becoming obsolete. In October 1986 the Seaman's Union marched in silent protest through the streets of Oslo. And then they got even more reason to protest.

In 1930 the shipowner Erling Dekke Naess had registered his whale factory *Viking* in Panama. This was for him the start of a glorious shipping career abroad. In the 50s and 60s his Panama-registered fleet was estimated to be the third largest in the world. His activities brought him recognition that varied from his being called 'Public Enemy Number One' and 'pirate', to the award of the Royal Order of St Olav, and an honorary doctorate of the University of Bergen. In a speech in Oslo in January 1984, he suggested that Norway set up her own international ship register. At this point the country still had a merchant fleet with a tonnage of about 32 million tons deadweight. The flight from the flag had started, but was not yet catastrophic.

Nobody then believed that such an improbable idea would ever become a reality in Norway! But in the autumn of 1986 the proposal was put in all seriousness before the annual general meeting of the shipowners' federation, and on 1 July 1987, the Norwegian International Ship Register (NIS) was established in Bergen at record speed, following the most bitter discord in Norway for many years. It gave shipowners the right to fire Norwegian seamen on NIS ships and to hire foreign seamen at Third World rates; it also granted tax exemption to foreign investors in NIS. Some 10,000 seamen were sacrificed in order to improve the health of Norwegian shipping.

The day after the register had been established, the first NIS registered ship, M/S *Norcan* of the Stenersen line, called at Bergen. The temporary Norwegian crew had been put ashore in Rotterdam the day before and replaced by Indians. "We can't afford Norwegians. They demand one month at sea and one ashore, while the Asians stay at sea for nine months and ask for less pay," said shipowner Sigmund Stenersen to a Bergen newspaper. The Indian crew members received 3,000 kroner a month, the Norwegian sailors got 8,600.

If not for the sailor, for the shipowner NIS was a big success. After three years, three-quarters of the Norwegian merchant fleet was registered in NIS, and Norway was again one of the most important shipping nations in the world. In May 1990, the fleet consisted of 1,460 vessels with a total 51.5 million tons deadweight. Of these, 837 ships (37.2 million tons deadweight) were registrered in the NIS, and only 262 ships (1.7 million tons deadweight) were in the national register and had kept their Norwegian crews. There were still 365 ships (12.6 tons deadweight) sailing under flags of convenience.

The Norwegian Seaman's Mission is now at a loss. Since 1864 it has provided Norwegian seamen with waffles and the Gospel, reading rooms and mail from home, in its many churches all over the world. There are still 23 of these, and there are no plans to phase them out. Some 2,000 seaman's mission societies, run by increasingly aged women, still send their Christmas gifts to young boys out in the unknown. Now the mission has new target groups: oil workers in the North Sea, students and Norwegian residents abroad. But there is hardly any use in sending parcels to Ola Nordmann the sailor. He is no longer to be found in the seaman's church. He is sitting at the Job Centre hoping for new work.

ECONOMIC TRENDS

CHAPTER TEN is about the Norwegian factory worker, about waterfalls and hydroelectricity, profits and losses,. and about industrial life that became so chaotic that no-one knew any longer who owned whom.

When Dad was young the factory was unchanging. It was somewhere he took his lunch box and thermos flask to every day, regular as clockwork, shift after shift, year after year, making something that had always been made there, for the very same owners and with the very same workmates. The factory was as solid as a rock. The Stock Exchange report on the radio was something you heard as an even, monotonous background noise while you had your afternoon nap, as stimulating as the weather report. And a savings bank was still the modest building in the station town or fishing village, founded by the village's grandparents and run in their spare time by the fathers.

But after the Oslo Stock Exchange had lived a quiet life on the outskirts of Europe for many years, it plunged into a wild rollercoaster ride in the unprecedented boom of the 1980s when newly rich financiers and old companies bought each other up right, left and centre, leaving no-one untouched. Directors who had always displayed wisdom and decorum in interviews, now presided over extraordinary general meetings in a climate 'tainted by mutual accusation, slander and mistrust as deep as the ocean'. A pack of young men in ties and loud-checked suits suddenly appeared, hot on the trail of the new money to be found in media companies and fashion retailing, estate agencies and industrial enterprises. Soup producers started making asphalt, mining companies published weekly magazines, shares changed hands so quickly that poor old Ola no longer knew who owned him when he came to the factory in the morning.

'Cannibals of the business world' was how former prime minister, Per Borten, described these new heroes of the Norwegian media age. The result of the Stock Exchange's wild go-go days was that the Government had to pass a new Stock Exchange Law, reinforcing public control of the activity and bringing in more rigorous punishment for offenders. Most people were relieved that the legislation came when it did. All these things happened just as Norway found herself in the oil age. In the 1980s it was hardly possible to give a survey of business and finance valid for more than one week!

122. In April the wood grouse, the biggest of the gallinaceous wild fowl, convene at their habitual mating places in old coniferous woods. (Pål Hermansen/Samfoto/NN)

123. In many bird colonies, the puffin is the dominant species. (Roger Engvik)

124. The hare enjoys itself when spring comes and the mountain birch is once more in leaf. (Pål Hermansen/ Samfoto/NN)

125. The marsh marigold (Caltha palustris) grows best in wet conditions, even in streams, such as this one on the Finnmarksvidda plateau. (Pål Hermansen/Samfoto/NN)

126. *The modest white anemone (Anemone nemorosa) grows in abundance in spring in many woodland glades.* (Pål Hermansen/ Samfoto/NN)

127. *Mountain plants burst into bloom in no time once the snow melts. The purple mountain saxifrage (Saxifraga oppossitifolia) blossoms as early as April.* (R. Frislid/NN)

128. The starry saxifrage (Saxifraga stellaris) thrives in the moist green moss on the mountainsides. (Pål Hermansen/Samfoto/NN)

129. Among the flowers adding colour
to the summer landscape is a variety
of harebells. This is Campanula
persicifelia. (Pål Hermansen
/Samfoto/NN)

130. Where old grazing land is no
longer exploited, wild flowers take
over, to be replaced in time by
woodland. (Pål Hermansen/Samfoto) ▷

The old Norsemen, like people in other countries, had to bring out the resources from wherever they were: fish from the sea, game from the moors, trees from the forest, and iron ore from the hillside. In the Viking age furs and pelts were the most important export articles, superseded by stockfish in the thirteenth century. As time went by, many settlements grew up where rivers met the sea, preferably where there was also another resource nearby.

Rivers and waterfalls are the salient features of the Norwegian landscape. The playful streams are where boys build mills, their own wooden turbines that whirl round and round. The waterfalls are mysterious, thundering, frightening, the home of the river sprite *Nøkken*, the creature of the underworld who teaches young boys to play the fiddle. It was not without reason that Ibsen let certain of his characters vanish into the waterfall.

The waterfall became the Norseman's prime helpmate in the centuries that followed, not least for grinding corn and cutting timber. Each farm had to have its own flourmill and sawmill. The water-driven sawmill first came into use in Norway in the sixteenth century. Soon vast amounts of timber products were being exported to England and the Netherlands, so much so that huge oak forests were destroyed in the south. There was a clear need for restriction, and in 1668 royal charters were granted to 664 sawmills to provide sawn timber for export. The others had permission to provide only for local needs.

Next came mining. In 1524 the first royal charter was given to a copper mine in Seljord in Telemark. Then came the silver mines, run by German mining experts brought to the country by the Danish king. They worked the Norwegian peasantry hard, and forced them to provide both coal and wood for the mines.

The Renaissance king, Christian IV, founded the ironworks at Bærum and Fossum near Oslo, the silverworks at Kongsberg and the copper industry of Røros. Eventually there were 15 ironworks, their names to be seen on iron stoves in old Norwegian houses.

In the distinctive mountain town of Røros, which is among the most worthy of conservation in Europe, huge slag heaps are a reminder of the miners' toil in the pits. The writer Johan Falkberget has immortalized their lives in his novels. The English social economist and population expert Thomas Robert Malthus travelled in Norway in 1799 and left this contemporary description of life in Røros:

"The miners work from Monday morning till Friday noon. In this period they live in a building near the mines, and on Friday they go home to their wives and children. If, by working extra hard, they finish the stipulated work before time, they can go home earlier. Usually they work from 4 a.m. until 5 p.m., except for meal times and for two hours from 10 to 12 . . . When we left the mine, we went to see the house where the miners are lodged during the week, and I think I have never seen more pitiable accommodation. Almost a hundred men are crammed together in a room that measures 8 × 9 yards. They sleep on narrow bunks in a kind of scaffolding that runs along the walls. The bunks looked no wider than two feet, and we saw neither bedding nor covering. Many of the men were sleeping as we entered the room. They never take off their clothes from Monday to Friday." These were Malthus's impressions, recorded in the light of a miner's lamp.

A century later he could have switched on the electric light.

Norway's first commercial hydroelectricity plant started up in Skien

131. By means of 12 mighty curves around waterfalls and ravines the Trollstigen road helps motorists to ascend 800 metres (2,600 feet) up the mountainside. This road in the Romsdalen district of western Norway, completed in 1936, took 20 years to build.
(Mittet)

in 1885. Hammerfest, the northernmost town in the world, was the firs
in the world to get electric street lights, in 1890. Our waterfalls have
made Norway, with its warm rooms and well-lit streets on a cold winter'
night, the country that consumes the most energy per capita in the
world. In 1983 each human being used on average under 2,000 kilowatt
hours of electricity a year. Yugoslavs used 3,000, West Germans 6,000
North Americans 10,000, Icelandics, Swedes and Canadians roughl
15,000 each. Norwegians used 22,000. Ola Nordmann does not turn of
the light when he leaves a room.

The encyclopædia *Nordisk Conversationslexicon* was not quite
correct when it pronounced in 1871 that electric light 'is hardly suitable
to use for ordinary illumination, as it is so expensive, and also so intense
that one contracts inflammation of the eye merely from seeing it fo
a few minutes'.

For a long time the development of hydroelectricity met no resist
ance whatsoever. The plants were small, the power was essential, the
future lay in electricity, and we all wanted it. But as the waterfall
disappeared and the sites made more and more unsightly scars on area
of outstanding natural beauty, people started to realize the value of wha
was being lost. Environmentalists intensified their protests in the 1960s
and Norway's largest waterfall and her great pride, Vøringsfossen, wa
partially saved. The watershed in the attitude to hydroelectric powe
development came around 1970, but the great battle was to be the figh
for the Alta-Kautokeino river ten years later.

Just after the Second World War there were 2,000 electricity plants
Since then only very large projects have been constructed. Today there
are 425 such plants in the country, producing 105 TerraWatt hour
a year (1 TWh = one thousand million kilowatt hours). Much of Norway'
water power is still unexploited. If everything were to be tapped, i
would be possible to reach an output of 550 TWh a year. In the mid-80s i
was reckoned that it would only pay to develop 172 TWh. At that poin
25 TWh were left untouched for environmental reasons. Experts esti
mate that from now on it will be cheaper to exploit the natural gas in the
North Sea than the remaining waterfalls.

Experiments have been made with wave power on the west coast
but this will hardly be significant before the turn of the century. Wind
power has been rejected as a possibility so far, but solar energy has been
tried out on a small scale. Any plans to develop nuclear power in Norway
were scrapped after the Chernobyl accident in the Soviet Union in 1986
No-one in Norway can tell you what is to replace the natural gas when i
runs out one day.

The true industrial revolution in Norway began in the 1850s, when
textile production started up by the Aker river in Oslo. Hjula Mill was the
best known. Wood pulp and chemical pulp factories were opened in
forestry areas. In Skien the Union company was started, and the Gren
land district came to be one of Norway's most densely populated and
most polluted areas. In 1891 Sarpsborg, using British capital, inaugu
rated its pulp and paper factory Borregaard, destined to be the pride o
Norwegian industry for a century to come.

The real bonanza in Norwegian industrial development was due to
another waterfall, Rjukanfossen. At a dinner party given by the future
prime minister, Gunnar Knudsen, in 1903, the engineer Sam Eyde and
professor Kristian Birkeland got talking. The former had access to a vas
supply of hydroelectric power. He had founded Elkem, an electrochemi

al company, and he was convinced that it would be possible to produce artificial fertilizer from nitrogen in the atmosphere, if only he could direct a flash of lightning, an electric flame fierce enough for the extraction process. Birkeland had just hit upon this – the previous week! The outcome was the founding in 1905 of the Norwegian hydroelectric nitrogen company that became Norsk Hydro, the taming of the spectacular Rjukan Falls, and the factories built in Notodden and Rjukan.

Needless to say, Rjukan, a small place at the bottom of Vestfjord valley under the towering Gausta peak, was rapidly transformed: its population had increased to 8,000 by 1920. Northern Europe's first passenger cableway was installed to lift people out of the narrow valley up into the light and air. The place flourished, people were happy and life went on – for some decades. Rjukan is most famous for the events that took place there on 27 February 1943, when the Norwegian Resistance sabotaged Norsk Hydro's heavy water plant in order to prevent Hitler from developing the atomic bomb.

More electrometallurgical and electrochemical plants were to be built in this country so rich in waterfalls. Vast plants with smelting furnaces and rolling-mills were squeezed into small communities, spewing their smoke up the hillsides and their waste products into the sea. Much of this industry produced iron alloys for reinforcing other metals. Some factories had private backing, others were state enterprises that aimed at keeping the population distributed throughout the country. The engineering industry was now well under way; the fish products and high technology industries were to follow.

The towns had their own specialities. Christian Bjelland made Stavanger into a sardine town, Helly J. Hansen made raincoats in Moss, Jonas Øgland bicycles in Sandnes, the Viking Company made rubber boots in Askim. The Sunnmørings make furniture, Mustad & Co. at Gjøvik sell fish-hooks all over the world, and Jordan's toothbrushes are exported to 80 countries, beaten on the market only by Colgate and Gillette. The toothpicks on Thai Airlines are made in the small forest village of Flisa in Solør.

Despite all this, in 1986 the government had to draw the conclusion that Norway is still a poorly developed industrial nation, mostly deliver-

Farmers fishing, drying and smoking salmon. Illustration to Olaus Magnus: 'History of the Nordic Peoples', Rome 1555.

ing semi-manufactures that are finished elsewhere. The raw material
brought here, where water-power is cheap, and sent on in an unfinishe
state. Nor is there much chance of expansion within the market. Th
leading industrial nations are now concentrating on brain power an
information technology. The semi-manufacturing countries are likely t
be left behind, exposed to fluctuations in the market, as many ra
material producers have been for a long time.

Norwegian industry has become more international in recent year
In 1985 the majority of shares in about 1,800 companies were in foreig
hands, while Norwegians had interests in 4,400 foreign companies a
over the world.

With traditional industries such as shipbuilding, fishing and minin
in decline, Ola Nordmann has had to look around for new ways of makin
a living, whether in fish farms, tourism, fashion, the media or computer
Sometimes it works, sometimes it does not. In many ways Norway is th
land of small firms. There are 181,000 of them, often run by one ma
and his wife. Some 40 per cent of production is accounted for by firm
employing less than 100 people.

However, it is the large companies that count! Listed according t
turnover, the largest firms in the mid-80s were Statoil, Norsk Hydr
Esso, Philips, the insurance company Storebrand-Norden, the state
owned telecommunications Televerket, Shell and Elf. The highest ne
profits were made by eight oil companies, followed by Den norsk
Creditbank and Televerket. Den norske Creditbank was later to suffe
heavy losses, not least through ill-judged placing of shares. Norsk Hydr
had the highest number of employees – 26,400, followed by the stat
postal service (25,100) and Televerket (21,200).

Among the world's largest companies outside the U.S.A., Statoil i
ranked number 78 and Norsk Hydro 101. Statoil is part of the oil chapte
in our saga of Norway and the Norwegians. And what happened to Nors
Hydro after that historic dinner in 1903, when the lightning flashe
between Sam Eyde and Kristian Birkeland? The process developed b
the two of them to extract artificial fertilizer from the air proved to be to
power-intensive, and was replaced at the end of the 1920s by th
German Haber-Bosch process. The Rjukan plant was rebuilt, and Norsl
Hydro created Norway's largest industrial works, Porsgrunn Fabrikke
on Herøya, in the Grenland area. In the 1960s electric power wa
replaced by oil, and the plant once more had to be tailored to mee
petrochemical-based production. Norsk Hydro became an oil compan
itself, started operating in the North Sea, bought up petrol stations, an
planned the production of gas.

Before the Second World War, Ardalstangen and Øvre Ardal wer
two peaceful, humble villages as far as you can get up the Sognefjord, a
the foot of Jotunheimen, surrounded by peaks of up to 1,300 metre
(over 4,000 feet) on all sides. During the war the German occupatio
forces started work on an aluminium plant there. After the war th
Norwegian State took over the unfinished project and carried on with th
Ardal plant, taking into account the population factor and the effect o
the small community. Ardal was a typical example of post-war industria
development in Norway.

Forty years later Ardal and Sunndal were amalgamated with th
aluminium division of Norsk Hydro, which already owned the smelting
works at Karmøy in the west. Hydro Aluminium became the secon
largest aluminium company in Europe, supplying 600,000 tons a year

with 50 plants at home and abroad, and a total workforce of 12,000 in 12 countries. In Norway the company controls the key industries of many small towns.

In addition, Norsk Hydro is behind the artificial fertilizer produced at Glomfjord in Nordland and in France, magnesium in Canada, fish farmed in Ireland, Iceland and Scotland, ammunition made at the Norwegian Dyno industries, the chocolate from Freia and Marabou, and a great deal else – with total assets of 41 billion kroner in 1985. The concern accounted for 17 per cent of the total value of the companies quoted on the Stock Exchange in 1986. The State owns 51 per cent of the shares, 10.4 are privately owned by Norwegians, and 38.6 by foreign investors. Yet the small town of Rjukan, where it all started, is now a dying community, unless it is to be artificially revived by hotels, motels and sportels, chalets and skilifts high up on the plateau beneath Gausta-toppen.

Norway's largest private industrial concern is Aker-Norcem, which started as a mechanical workshop in 1842 and a cement plant in 1892, and now has a workforce of 14,000 and a turnover of 10 billion kroner a year. Its entrepreneurial activities range over the whole world, and it has helped to make concrete platforms for the oil rigs in the North Sea, through Norwegian Contractors.

Illustration to 'Three in Norway by Two of Them' by J.A. Lees and W.J. Clutterbuck, 1882.

The Kværner business, opened in 1848 by the brothers Jens and Andreas Jensen as Myrens Workshop in an old smithy near Akerselva in Oslo, is one of the world's largest makers of hydroelectric turbines, a pioneer in wave power, and supplier to the oil industry, in particular through Rosenberg Verft in Stavanger.

Elektrisk Bureau employs 10,000 people in 17 different plants in Norway, has interests in 12 countries, and touches every Norwegian directly – through his telephone.

Elkem, which branched out from Christiania Spigerverk and the company founded by Sam Eyde in 1904, produces steel, ferro-alloys, aluminium and many kinds of manufactured goods in 25 different places in Norway, from Finnmark to Lista.

Borregaard has now become Orkla-Borregaard and produces everything from chemical pulp and paper to washing powder, biscuits, sausages and women's magazines, and it is one of the big shareholders in the Norwegian newspaper world.

Norwegian state enterprises do not exactly flourish. Not that there are many of them. Some were established for defence reasons: the armaments factory at Kongsberg in 1814, the Horten naval shipyard in 1849, and the Raufoss munitions factory in 1896. After the last world war it became vital for Norway to be self-sufficient in steel. The State therefore bought a substantial part of the mining company A/S Sydvaranger in Kirkenes, on the Soviet border.

Norway's really great national effort was the founding of A/S Norsk Jernverk, the ironworks in Mo i Rana, a small town that after the war had a population of 9,000. The idea was to make use of the raw materials from the Rana mines, take in coal from Svalbard, give the northerners something to keep them in the area; in fact it was to be the epitome of industrial development according to all the principles of social democracy.

The town grew big and strong, thanks to the iron foundry, and it gradually increased in size to 26,000 inhabitants. Of these, 5,500 were directly employed by the ironworks in the middle of the 70s, and the whole town of Mo was dependent on it. The State owned 80 per cent of the shares, Elkem 20 per cent.

But the ironworks made a loss. Over a period of five years alone the State had to contribute three billion kroner to keep it going, despite the company having laid off a thousand men in the same period. In 1989 the production of ore-based iron stopped in Mo, after 30 years. Now it is only in Svalbard that the authorities have no qualms about subsidizing the mines. They are essential to maintaining our sovereignty in the north.

The State is loosening its grip on many state-owned companies. Televerket has been divided into two parts, one a monopoly, the other competitive. The state broadcasting company Norsk Rikskringkasting has become an independent body, and the postal service is also to be given economic freedom. Conservative politicians wish to sell off Norsk Hydro to private investors – so far without luck.

At the start of the 90s, it must be conceded that the idea of solidarity is not as widespread in social democracy as it was in the hard years after the war. Today it is profit that counts. Norway now has the highest level of unemployment since the depression years of the 30s.

News reports on corruption have become a part of our daily life, not least in the capital, where in 1990 the lord mayor had to withdraw after being criticized for mixing private and municipal interests.

The Norwegians have lost their innocence, if they ever had any.

STRIKING IT RICH

*CHAPTER ELEVEN tells the tale of Ola Nordmann
who turned into an oil tycoon, and how Americans
and Spaniards, Portuguese and Mexicans helped
him to get oil out of the North Sea.*

Ever since the day Edwin L. Drake first struck oil in Pennsylvania in 1859, petroleum had been something remote from the average Norwegian. To seamen who shipped the oil, from Texas and Abadan, it was a reality, but for the landlubber petrol was something in a can, maybe in a tank, to heat cold houses in the winter. The paraffin barrel on its rack in the garden was part of the Norwegian scene.

But then, in the late 1960s, someone claimed to have found oil in the North Sea! Since then, Norwegians have been fed with a daily diet of information about sectors and drilling, rigs and OPEC meetings.

Norway has three per cent of the gas reserves and 1.5 per cent of the oil reserves in the world — on her doorstep, so to speak. The oil adventure has completely changed Norwegian ideas about industry and has made young men aim at a career 'in oil' instead of at sea.

We started south of the 62nd parallel and constructed a big, floating 'city' far south in the North Sea, Ekofisk, and another just outside Bergen, Statfjord. There are many large and small oilfields between them. In 1986 oil and gas were produced from 12 fields in all in the North Sea by means of 19 production platforms and a sea-bed construction. Many fields have not yet been exploited, such as the large Troll field that in a few years' time will supply half Europe with natural gas. By 1987 it was estimated that all the oil and gas south of the 62nd parallel had been recorded and the search for oil has since moved further north. On the Haltenbanken shelf, off mid-Norway, a large deposit of gas has been found. The big question now is how much is yet to be discovered in the Barents Sea and on Svalbard.

Ola Nordmann was sceptical in 1962 when foreigners turned up wanting to investigate what was at the bottom of the North Sea. The background to this was that gas had been found in the Netherlands. "Search, but don't drill," the Norwegians said at the beginning. But in 1965 the first permission to drill was granted.

Norway had by then proclaimed her sovereignty over the Norwegian Continental Shelf and the North Sea had been divided between Norway, Denmark and Great Britain according to a centre-line principle.

In the summer of 1966 the first hole was drilled on the Norwegian

Continental Shelf. It was dry. But 1968 saw the first commercially exploitable find on the Cod field. On 23 December 1969, the Ekofisk field was discovered, and in 1971 the first well was put into production. The oil adventure had really begun.

But the Norwegians had no idea what to do when they were suddenly thrown into the oil age. Even if they could transport the oil, they couldn't get it up from the sea-bed. Consequently, 91 per cent of the projects were handled by foreigners, and foreigners were wholly responsible for operations when the first sectors were divided up. It was Spaniards, Portuguese and Mexicans who developed Ekofisk. Until 1970 Norway had to import ordinary workers as well as experts. The Norwegians had enough to do coping with the on-shore industry. In the mid-80s all the production fields were still being operated by foreign companies. The North Sea was a new Texas! To make up for this the Norwegians gave the fields names taken from Norse mythology and folk tales.

As early as 1969 the government had claimed the right to a share in all the commercially exploitable fields on the Norwegian Shelf. In 1972 the Norwegian Petroleum Directorate and the state oil company Statoil were established to take charge of all the Norwegian interests. As time went by the Norwegians took an increasingly active part.

The first finds created a real Klondyke atmosphere in Norway. Everyone wanted to buy shares, everyone wanted to speculate in the 'black gold' of the sea. But it soon turned out to be more difficult than anticipated to raise the capital and acquire the know-how for the enormously expensive production. The way most Norwegians benefited from the oil bonanza was not from gains on the Stock Exchange but indirectly, through the general increase in revenue brought in by Statoil. The comments of the director of Statoil became almost as significant as those of the prime minister — perhaps because we did not hear him so often.

In the twenty years that have gone by since the start, Statoil has grown into one of Scandinavia's leading industrial concerns with about 10,000 on the payroll. It pumps up 50 million tons of oil a year, and is involved in some way in everything that goes on in the North Sea. Statoil is the operator of the Statfjord and Gullfaks fields, runs the gigantic Statepipe system, and is responsible for shipping the crude oil from Statfjord; it runs the refineries at Mongstad and at Bamble, it has bought up about a thousand petrol stations in Denmark and Sweden, and controls 27 per cent of the Norwegian market.

The other great Norwegian oil company, Norsk Hydro, created from the giant company founded by Sam Eyde and Kristian Birkeland in 1905, is 51 per cent state-owned. The company has been involved in the North Sea since the beginning of the oil adventure, in particular in the Ekofisk, Frigg and Gullfaks fields. It owns a large part of the great petro-chemical installations at Bamble in Telemark, runs petrol stations in Sweden, and is involved in the planning of a vast gas power station in the west of Norway.

The only privately-owned Norwegian company found fit to operate on the Norwegian Shelf is Saga Petroleum. But despite its 55,000 shareholders, it has been unable to manage without considerable help from industry. The Swedish mega company Volvo owns 20 per cent of the shares, and Saga wishes to increase foreign investment to 40 per cent. Appropriately, it is Saga that is to expand the Snorre field. After all, it was Snorre who gave Norway the sagas!

135. Goats know the art of exploiting steep pastures. Communal dairy farms with hundreds of animals ensure that Norwegians get their supply of the traditional brown goat's cheese. (Johan Brun/NN)

136. Large flocks of sheep are taken into the mountains in summer to feed on the verdant pastures during the two or three months this bonanza will last. (Johan Brun/NN)

137. When the sheep return from the highland pastures in the autumn, all other traffic must give way. (Helge Sunde/Samfoto)

138

138. The Fjording is still used for agricultural purposes. Though mostly replaced by machines, the horse is holding its ground on small farms. (Husmo-Foto)

139. On farms in western Norway
with their steep slopes, the sturdy
little Fjording is almost indispensable.
(Husmo-Foto)

140. The wood-burning stove and the coffee pot have a very important place in the small huts which used to be the home of forestry workers for most of the week. Today, new roads make it possible for them to drive daily to the forests. (Husmo-Foto)

141. Grey, weather-beaten log cabins with turf roofs are typical of the old dairy farm. But the equipment hanging on the wall shows that the milking machine has found its way even here. (R. Frislid/NN)

142. Modern forestry is based on clear felling of larger or smaller areas, which appreciably alters the appearance of woodlands. (Pål Hermansen/Samfoto/NN)

143. Upland dairy farms are still worked in some places. Hay from such farms is an important supplement to winter fodder. This dairy farm is at Innfjorden, in the western district of Romsdalen. (R. Frislid/NN)

144. Forested hills are typical of the scenery in the interior of eastern Norway, as here near Lake Krøderen. (R. Frislid/NN) ▷

There is also a third private company, the Norwegian Petroleum Company. When oil fever was at its height, it had to hire the largest cinema in Oslo to conduct its annual general meetings. It is still one of the companies with the largest number of shares on the Oslo Stock Exchange (58,000 in all), but it showed a loss in 1986, when the shares were worth only half their nominal value and the company waited in vain for a chance to operate in Norwegian territorial waters.

Anyone who flies over the North Sea will see that production platforms vary. Steel platforms were the first to be used. To ensure stability, supports, 50 to 100 metres (140–280 feet) in length, were thrust down into the sea-bed from the platform legs. Gravity-base structures are another type, usually great concrete platforms held in place by their own weight. The most famous of these are the Norwegian-constructed Condeep platforms, the first of which was placed in a depth of 70 metres (200 feet) on the Ekofisk field in 1970. But operations at greater depths require new kinds of platform, one type being a floating steel platform attached to the sea-bed by a length of steel tubing. Saga Petroleum is planning to use this type of platform on the Snorre field, due to go into production from 1992. It is already in operation on the British Hutton field in the North Sea.

Technical developments have also made it possible to eliminate the production platform. A system of this kind is used on North East Frigg. The so-called production valves are placed in a steel frame on the sea-bed, and production is operated from a control platform that receives radio signals from the Frigg field. This may be the future pattern of oil development in the Barents Sea, a development that is hardly visible on the surface, unlike the steel and concrete cities that populate the North Sea.

Three types of raw material are obtained: dry gas (methane gas with small parts of ethane and propane), wet gas (ethane, propane and butane gas) and crude oil.

Oil and gas are brought ashore partly by ship, partly through pipelines on the sea-bed. The tankers fuel from loading buoys connected to the production platforms. These loading buoys are vast, the one at Statfjord A being 182 metres (654 feet) high. The pipelines have a diameter of up to 125 centimetres (36 inches) and convey oil to most countries around the North Sea.

From Ekofisk the oil is piped to Teesside in England and the natural gas to Emden in West Germany. The gas goes from Frigg in two parallel gas pipes to St Fergus in Scotland. From Murchison the wet gas and oil is taken to Sullom Voe in the Shetlands and the dry gas to St. Fergus. In the autumn of 1986, Prime Minister Gro Harlem Brundtland officially inaugurated the Statepipe system, Norway's most ambitious industrial project as well as the world's greatest offshore transport system for gas, and the main artery connecting the North Sea both to Norway and to the pipelines of the Continent. The pipeline stretches 880 kilometres (550 miles) under the sea.

Yet another vast pipeline is to be laid in the 1990s, from the rich fields of Troll and Sleipner to Zeebrugge in Belgium, altogether 830 kilometres (515 miles), or 1,300 (810 miles) if you count all the side lines that lead the oil off to the various customers: Ruhrgass, BEB and Thyssengas in Germany, Gasunie in Holland, Distrigaz in Belgium, and Gaz de France.

Back on shore the Norwegians are constantly aware of the oil. Huge

145. Autumn and late winter are times for felling timber. Forestry is an important industry in Norway: up to 10 million cubic metres (13 million cubic yards) of timber are cut each year. (A. Normann/ Samfoto)

rigs are towed in and out of the fjords, old-established shipyards are wiped off the map or remodelled to serve the oil industry, and small villages are transformed into industrial sites. The most intensive activity takes place in Stavanger, Norway's oil city, which has 150,000 people living within half an hour's drive of the city centre. The old brisling town now has the highest house prices in Norway, since 10 international and two Norwegian companies are based there. Oil tanks and pipelines have proliferated in many other places: Slagentangen in Vestfold, Rafnes in Bamble, Sola in Rogaland, Mongstad in North Hordaland.

The oil refinery in Mongstad, now owned by Statoil, started up in 1975 and is capable of supplying tankers of up to 300,000 tons. For Statoil's new crude oil terminal there, 2.6 million cubic metres (53 million cu.ft.) of stone have to be blasted out of the rock — the same amount that went to the building of the Cheops pyramid in Egypt. The terminal and the refinery together make it the country's greatest land-based industrial project ever, originally estimated to cost 7 billion kroner. It is to receive 90 per cent of all the oil from the Statfjord and Gullfaks fields, and will supply all Statoil's petrol stations, which sell one out of five gallons of petrol sold in Scandinavia.

But in 1987 the Mongstad project turned into Norway's greatest industrial scandal when it was found to have exceeded the building estimate by 5 billion kroner, an amount so astronomical that the wits of the press immediately introduced a new monetary unit, 'the mong'!

The great Statepipe system goes ashore in Kårstø, which has become one of Norway's busiest ports with 250 ships calling in each year. The North Sea gas is brought in here and the wet gas is separated and sent on to the U.S.A., Sweden and other countries. The dry gas is transported to Ekofisk and from there by pipeline to Emden in West Germany.

Now Statoil, in co-operation wilth the state-run company Statskraft, is to build a gas-fuelled power station at Kårstø, while Norsk Hydro plans another at Karmøy. The oil from Oseberg is to be brought ashore further up the west coast, at Sture in Øygarden. A third gas power station is to be built in mid-Norway, based on Haltenbanken gas, and a gas pipe is likely to be extended into Sweden, which is committed to phasing out its nuclear power stations by the year 2010.

In short, Ola Nordmann is claiming more and more of the oil action. In 1977 there were 27,500 people involved in oil production offshore and on land. Of these, 21 per cent were foreigners. In 1987 the number had

Illustration (by the authors) to 'Three in Norway by Two of Them' by J.A. Lees and W.J. Clutterbuck, 1882.

increased to 64,300 while the number of foreigners had fallen to six per cent. On 29 January 1987, a red letter day in Norwegian oil history, Ola Nordmann was able to send out the first 100 per cent Norwegian-produced barrel of oil from the Gullfaks A platform. It had been planned and constructed by Norwegians under the combined ownership of three Norwegian companies: Statoil, Saga and Norsk Hydro. It was also the first rig to have Norwegian as the working language.

Until the mid 1980s all was well in the oil country of Norway. The 'black gold' flowed, the gas poured out, investments were huge (33 billion in 1986), but so were returns. The standard of living reached a new peak, and unemployment was among the lowest in Europe. Ola Nordmann took off to the Canaries for his holidays and traded in his old Volvo for the latest model. Then he was jolted into remembering that he was not alone in the world! There was a drastic fall in the internationally-set oil price, upon which he had based all his activities. Fluctuations in oil income signalled the danger of being solely dependent upon this industry. Nor does oil and fossil fuel last for ever. At the present rate of exploitation, the Norwegian oil bonanza should be over by the turn the century. If the companies are allowed to have their way, 75 per cent of the oil reserves will have run out by that time. However, we do have enough gas (almost half the total reserves of Europe) to last another century. It is highly probable that Norway has reserves of up to 10 billion tons of oil equivalents, including those in the Barents Sea. But the waters of the north are among the most rigorous in the world, with severe winter storms, continuous darkness and an exceedingly harsh climate. Exploitation will be very costly.

The north of Norway felt sadly left behind in the oil age. It was therefore a subject of general rejoicing when the Norwegian sector of the Barents Sea was cleared for drilling in 1987 and when the government that same year gave out the first three concessions in the Barents Sea to Statoil, Norsk Hydro and Saga Petroleum. At last north Norway was to get its share of the riches. At last people would stop moving away!

The Russians had been drilling for oil and gas in the Barents Sea from the early 80s and begun production in 1987. In June of that year, Ross Rig started exploratory drilling in the Norwegian sector. A month later the first sample was seen on the deck, brought up from 1,000 metres deep in the Finnmark West field, and Saga Petroleum could announce its find. It smelled of oil! Some days later, though, it proved to smell more of gas. And it is still not worth extracting gas so far north.

Oil has brought great riches to Norway, and also great unhappiness. The worst disaster happened on 27 March 1980, when the Alexander L. Kielland hotel platform toppled over into the sea, taking 124 people with it. Only 89 were saved.

One special danger is uncontrolled blow-outs on the rigs. The first occurred on 22 April 1977, when the oil burst up like a geyser spurting 60 metres (200 feet) into the air from the Bravo platform. The 100 men on board were evacuated. After a week the American 'well-killer' Red Adair managed to stop the blow-out. The environmental organization Greenpeace has published a report showing that a blow-out not stopped within 100 days would cause pollution to the Norwegian coastline costing between two and five billion kroner.

It is tempting to speculate about what is to be done with all the rigs when the oil adventure is over. It will cost 75 billion kroner just to remove the platforms from Ekofisk and Statfjord.

INTERNATIONAL ASPECTS

CHAPTER TWELVE tells us what it is like to be new in a foreign land, how Ola and Kari Nordmann get on in international company, and how they try to hold on to their culture.

Norway – for Norwegians?

The Norwegians' relationship to the rest of the world is somewhat complicated. Maybe not so much when we travel, as when the rest of the world comes to us. We aren't used to that at all. Up to the Second World War Norway lay secluded and totally innocent of all involvement. That whole villages in Finnmark were Finnish did not concern the south at all: Finnmark was so far away, and the Finns were inconspicuous. They were, after all, white. And Lapps were only something you read about in romantic novels. Around 1950 there were only two black people domiciled in Norway: one a drummer, the other a singer. Thirty years on, Norwegian papers were filled daily with stories of refugees and racial prejudice, and 32 nations were represented on the staff of the Grand Hotel in Oslo alone!

Once upon a time the Norwegian himself experienced what it was like to be an immigrant. Between 1825, when Cleng Persson led the first batch of immigrants from Rogaland on the sloop *Restauration,* and 1930, over 850,000 Norwegians set out for America. In the peak year of 1882, as many as 28,804 left the barren rocks of Norway to seek their fortune in 'God's own country'. The majority settled in the Mid-West, Minnesota and North Dakota, which are dotted with Norwegian place names. They also went to Texas, Seattle and Brooklyn in New York. They built Norwegian churches, and produced Norwegian newspapers – over 400 of these, some of them still in existence. Even if they were immigrants, they kept their identity and were proud of their origins. It was of course a matter of some irritation that there were already people there who owned the land: those 'obnoxious heathens' who would not let themselves be driven away, 'cannibals' perpetrating 'unspeakable acts of violence', as the Norwegians wrote home in their letters from America in the nineteenth century. It evokes unmistakable echoes of the descriptions the Vikings gave of the *Skrælingers* in Vinland 800 years earlier: ''They were black, ugly creatures, with ugly hair on their hands, wide eyes and broad faces.''

When Peter Minuit, governor of the colony of New Holland, bought Manhattan in 1626 to found New Amsterdam (later New York), it was a Norwegian – Cornelius Sand – who served as his interpreter in the ransaction that cost a few beads and baubles. Where the Indians hunted or buffalo there now live almost as many people with a Norwegian eritage as there are in Norway itself. In Seattle Norwegians fish in the ld fishing places of the native Americans. The white man and his wife id not arrive there until 1851.

The Norwegian found his place in the world, but did he accept preigners in return? The Constitution of 1814 stated that 'Jews are still anned from entering the country'. This clause was not removed until 851, after persistent campaigning by the poet and human rights activist enrik Wergeland. But even when Jews were allowed in, not everybody rished them welcome.

"To a great extent these Jews make a living from illicit trading, ainly in clocks, and partly through card games. They are people ithout a nation although they have been in Norway for many years... can only suppose that most of them can be bought for whatever urposes providing they get money from it." This was a confidential note om a policeman to the Norwegian Ministry of Justice during the First Vorld War.

Around 400 refugees came into Norway between the wars, although ere is a memo from the Ministry stating that 'in principle our policy is close the borders to refugees. If we relax this, we will have a host of em upon us'.

There are several special reasons why Norway ought to have positive policy on this issue. One is Fridtjof Nansen, the humanist and blar scientist who in 1921 was appointed the first High Commissioner r Refugees. Under his leadership, assistance was extended to 450,000 fugees and displaced persons after the First World War. He also helped indreds of thousands of Russians who had fled the Revolution. All ese people were saved thanks to a piece of paper that bore his name the Nansen passport. Another reason is that tens of thousands of orwegians themselves had to escape the country during the German cupation, making their way to Sweden, Britain, the U.S.A. and else-here.

Today there are between 15 and 23 million refugees in the world. ome 16,000, from 70 national groups in all, have been admitted to orway since the Second World War. About 1,500 foreigners, mainly les, chose to stay on in Norway when the war ended. Two years later 50 Jewish refugees came from camps in Germany and Poland. After the ungarian Rising we took in 1,500 Hungarian refugees, joined in recent ears by many Asians, mainly Vietnamese, but also Tamils and Iranians. f the Latin Americans, many are from Chile.

Norway is the Scandinavian country that has accepted the lowest imber of refugees: in 1985 we admitted 774 asylum-seekers, while the anes took in 10,000 and Sweden 15,000. In 1987 the number had risen 8,500. Since then Norway has passed a controversial Aliens Law that far more restrictive but should not affect 'genuine' refugees. Once dmitted, they will enjoy greater legal protection through the new gislation, but only a quarter of those who apply can count on getting olitical asylum. In 1986 almost 60 per cent were admitted on humanita-an grounds. This group must from now on reckon on being sent out of e country. Norway has, however, committed herself to taking in 1,000 nited Nations quota refugees.

The State set up a separate Aliens Office on 1 January 1988, at the me time establishing new reception centres for refugees in Oslo,

Kristiansand, Bergen, Trondheim and Stavanger. The idea is for these centres to hand over refugees to the care of local communities, who will be refunded up to a certain level. In practice, very few local authorities are willing to accept them, and indeed no-one seems prepared for the task. In the meantime there are 1,000 refugees waiting to be placed.

Some locations are considered unsuitable for refugees even though they offer housing and jobs. Båtsfjord, a fishing village in the far north of Finnmark, was turned down when it asked for 10 refugees, even though people from Finnmark are generous and used to seeing new faces. After all, people from all over the world come to work in its Båtsfjord fish factory — in 1987, 20 nations were represented! But the refugee secretariat said 'no' because Finnmark is so far north and the Tamils, from so far south, might feel out of place on the wharf in a snowstorm. However, the minister of social affairs intervened personally and Båtsfjord was sent its refugees — who are doing fine!

The local social workers who have to handle the cases lack the necessary knowledge about the refugees' background and culture. Nor do they have the time and resources to see that the refugees are trained or given a job. In consequence many have simply ended up living on welfare. If they get a job it is rarely compatible with their qualifications. A study made in 1980 showed that 32 per cent of university-trained Africans and 22 per cent of Latin Americans worked in shops, petrol stations, etc. in Oslo, as against only three per cent of Norwegian university graduates.

Many asylum-seekers have to wait months for a decision as to where they are to be placed, and are meanwhile lodged in hotels and boarding houses all over the country.

In 1986 400 reports of racial discrimination were made to the Anti-Racism Centre in Oslo. Many of these were clearly cases of institutional racism, some even involving the police. The police headquarters in Oslo received nearly 100 reports of racism, but all the cases were dismissed. The first encounter a refugee has with Norway is often with the immigration control at Fornebu Airport near Oslo, which in recent years has come in for a good deal of criticism.

Racist agitation increased in the late 80s and the papers were full of letters expressing prejudice towards immigrants. Incidents were reported in many parts of the country, including the Hedmark village of Brumunddal, where a Pakistani had his shop blown up by racist youths.

These negative examples are not the whole story. Not all Norwegians are racially prejudiced. On the contrary, there are always people ready to defend anyone who is discriminated against. But the Gallup polls show that Ola and Kari Nordmann may not be as tolerant as they make out. 'Norway — mainly for Norwegians' was how Aftenposten summed up the results of a poll on immigrants in 1985. A later opinion poll showed that 51 per cent of Norwegians did not think the country should accept more than the 6,000 refugees stipulated for the year. Only eight per cent were in favour of receiving more.

Some come, others go. In 1986, 16,211 Norwegians took up residence abroad. At the same time 23,383 foreigners moved here, over half of them Europeans. In 1987 there were altogether 115,000 foreigners in Norway, mainly Danes, Britons and Swedes, but also 8,000 Pakistanis.

Norway introduced an immigration ban in 1975. However, the experts point out that without immigration Norway will have a population of only 3.5 million by the year 2050, as against 4.1 million today.

With net immigration of 4,000 a year, by 2050 we will arrive at the same level as Sweden has today. In Sweden every tenth citizen is an immigrant.

Aid to developing countries increased from 9.6 million kroner in 1962 to 6.2 billion kroner in 1987. Norway provides 1.5 per cent of the total aid given in the world. And recent investigations prove that 85 per cent of the people are in favour of this. If we compare figures for 1984, we find that Norway contributed 1.2 per cent of her Gross National Product to development aid, the Netherlands did the same, while Denmark gave 0.85, Sweden 0.80, France 0.36, Great Britain 0.33 and the U.S.A. 0.24 per cent.

While Norwegians have long maintained close, and mostly amicable ties with their Scandinavian neighbours, before *glasnost* and *perestroika* they were almost without contact with their next-door neighbour in the north, the Soviet Union. Once in a while there was a tourist trip over the border, across the Pasvik River. There was not much traffic on a higher level either. When the Norwegian prime minister visited the Soviet Union in 1986, she was the first premier to do so since 1974. Nor had any of her Soviet counterparts been here between 1971, when Alexei Kosygin came to Norway, and 1988, when Prime Minister Ryshkov paid a visit.

But then things began changing very fast; the frontier was opened to a certain extent, and people started visiting one another. In 1990, President Mikhail Gorbachev was awarded the Nobel Peace Prize!

Yet from the other direction, from the mighty nation across the Atlantic, an unprecedented stream of influences pours into the small houses in the Pasvik Valley every minute of the day, in the form of sounds and images, cartoons and news flashes, rock music and mass-produced daydreams from Denver, Colorado.

Norwegians have not always felt at ease, squeezed between two superpowers. Not that many people normally go around thinking about the military situation. Though Norway has always been a loyal member of NATO, she has opposed the establishment of military bases, and the storage of nuclear warheads on her territory in peacetime.

Norway has her own mobilization forces in case of emergency. These consist of 325,000 men, or 7.7 per cent of the population, the highest number in any NATO nation. There are only 1,000 enlisted soldiers in the Norwegian Army, most of them serving with the United Nations contingent in the Middle East.

When Ola Nordmann is nineteen years old he has to do military service, twelve months in the Army, or fifteen in the Navy or Air Force. Conscientious objection to military service is possible on certain grounds, and 2,500 young people every year do alternative civil service.

The 'knorr', a shorter and beamier vessel than the Viking warship, the 'dakkar', was used by Viking explorers and settlers of Iceland, Greenland and North America. About 20 metres (50 feet) in length, it could carry some 30 people and a few head of livestock.

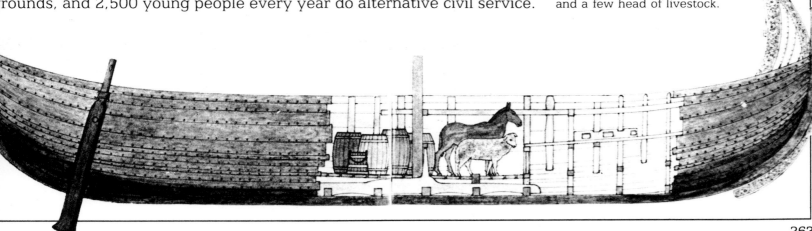

146. Norway at one time had some 750 stave churches, only 30 of which still exist. This one at Eidsborg (Telemark county) probably dates from the late 13th century. The porch and the shingle roof are typical of stave churches. (R. Frislid/NN)

There are about 21,400 national servicemen in Norway. Until they are forty-four they will have to put up with being summoned periodically for refresher training and sleeping in a tent, unless they are transferred to the Home Guard. An extension of the resistance movement against the Germans in the Second World War, the Home Guard consists of 90,000 men from all over the country, who would be sent to engage in guerilla warfare in an emergency. Equipped with loaded AG-3 guns, they meet every year for six days' training.

The Chernobyl nuclear disaster, on 26 April 1986, awakened Norway abruptly. In the event, the fallout reached Norway only after two days, but no-one knew how to cope with the situation. Contradictory statements were issued by the authorities and experts, many of them intended to comfort and reassure the general public. There is still a measure of disagreement among the experts. Some of them concluded that the effects had not been dramatic in Norway, and that it was quite safe to eat reindeer meat containing 20,000 becquerels, as long as one did not eat too much. Four years later, a high level of radioactivity was still to be found in sheep and reindeer. In 1990, farmers in some areas had to feed 150,000 sheep a special diet for up to eight weeks before slaughter to reduce the content in the meat to 600 becquerels.

But threats to the environment and human health appeared long before Chernobyl. For too many years Norway has been used as a dumping ground for industrial waste from the Continent and the British Isles. Thousands of lakes have had all life destroyed by acid rain. There are 400,000 freshwater lakes in Norway, covering an area that is larger than the farmland. As late as the 1950s, there were fish in every brook and pond, and small boys could catch them with their bare hands. Now the lakes of southern Norway have been polluted with sulphuric acid, 90 per cent of which comes from outside the country's borders.

A United Nations report in 1987 held Great Britain responsible for 43 per cent of the sulphuric pollution in the south of Norway and 36 per cent of the carbon dioxide. Even in the north of Norway British industry is the second greatest cause of pollution, appreciably ahead of local industry in this respect.

The sea will perhaps soon be as moribund as the rivers and lakes. In 1986 half the seaweed off the coast stretching from Nordmøre to Finnmark proved to be dead. If this continues we face an environmental catastrophe and a threat to both the fish and the human population of the coast.

During the great algae disaster in the summer of 1988, millions of fish died in their hatcheries and out in the Skagerrak and North Sea, and thousands of dead seals floated in to land. The German rivers Rhine, Elbe and Mosel alone carry 38 million tons of zinc, 13,500 tons of lead, 5,600 tons of copper and varying amounts of arsenic, cadmium, mercury and even radioactive waste into the sea every year, according to the American journal Newsweek's survey of the disaster. In addition, 145 million tons of ordinary sewage are dumped every year.

The Norwegians themselves are not free from blame. Because of discharge from Norwegian industry, 18 Norwegian fjords are heavily polluted. The worst hit are Iddefjorden near Halden and Kristiansand harbour and fjord. Health authorities in these areas warned people not to eat fish or seafood. Sørfjorden in Hardanger had already been labelled the stretch of water with the highest metal content in the world. At the end of this narrow fjord lies Odda, one of those Norwegian industrial

147. At North Cape, the midnight sun is visible about two and half months a year, from mid-May to the end of July. (Husmo-Foto) ▷

148. *The porch of a stave church is usually supported by carved wooden pillars, as at Hopperstad church, Sogn, western Norway.* (R. Frislid/NN)

149. *Stave churches are usually ornamented with elaborate woodcarving. This is a detail from Vågåmo church in the Gundbrandsdalen valley.* (R. Frislid/NN)

150. *Although rebuilt, Vågåmo stave church has retained many of its original details.* (R. Frislid/NN)

151

151. At the abandoned Eidsfoss iron works (Vestfold county), workers' houses which are nearly 200 years old have been restored, one of them providing premises for the local post office. (R. Frislid/NN)

152. A representative of one of the old Norwegian horse breeds, teh Nordland horse, feeding among boulders along the shore. (R. Frislid/NN)

152

153. On the traditional Norwegian farm, each building serves its own specific purpose. The number of structures on a farm can therefore become quite large even on a smaller farm, such as this one at Heidal in the Gudbrandsdalen valley. (R. Frislid/NN)

154. The church is usually the main landmark of the parish, like this medieval church at Norderhov, Ringerike. (R. Frislid/NN)

155. Old houses at Lærdalsøra on Sogne fjord, an ancient market place which is now a centre of tourism and salmon fishing. (R. Frislid/NN)

156. For very many Norwegians living in or near the coast, summer means boating. The traditional wooden motorboat is still very much in use. (R. Frislid/NN)

156

157. *A wedding in accordance with ancient custom in Heddal stave church, the largest church of this type in the country.* (S. E. Dahl/Samfoto)

158. *A rural wedding in traditional style, with folk dancing and the couple dressed in their local costumes, in Heddal, Telemark county.* (S. E. Dahl/Samfoto)

159. *The local folk costume, the* bunad, *is obligatory when celebrating a traditional peasant wedding, where the guests are served at long tables.* (S. E. Dahl/Samfoto) ▷

Tiden som er lagt tilbake

160

160. The churches of the mountain
and forest communities usually occupy
an imposing site, even if they are not
very impressive in size and
architecture. From Sollia in the east
Norwegian valley of Østerdalen.
(R. Frislid/NN)

*161. People tend to move from
isolated communities to more populous
places, and many small farms are left
abandoned today, particularly in
northern Norway, as here at
Ballangen, Nordland county.*
(R. Frislio/NN)

owns that grew up where freshwater ran into the sea. For years the zinc plant Norzink spewed 100,000 tons of heavy metal waste into the sea annually, although now its waste matter is transported to huge rock caverns. The Norwegian share in the company is in fact modest: Norzinc is owned by the Swedish firm Boliden and the British BP International, and most of the produce is exported. For the small community of 8,000 inhabitants the factory is, of course, of vital importance, but industrial jobs have a price. By now it is impossible to cultivate shellfish anywhere in the entire Hardanger fjord.

Not all pollution comes from the south. The Soviet nickel works, built in Nikel only six kilometres (3.7 miles) from the Norwegian border, is slowly killing the environment around Kirkenes and in the beautiful and fertile Pasvik Valley in Finnmark. The factory pumps out more noxious sulphur dioxide than the total of emissions by Norwegian industry – up to 320,000 tons a year. The inhabitants of the Pasvik Valley have recorded scorched trees, rust and dead moss and lichen, the staple food of reindeer. The people of Finnmark fear for their salmon rivers, and both Neiden and Grense Jacobselv are on the danger list.

One would imagine that at least Svalbard, 'the land of icy coast', had a clean bill of health, but the spectre of pollution has arrived there too. The clean Arctic winter is a myth. The Norwegian Institute of Air Pollution concluded in 1987, after five years of research, that Svalbard has as much sulphur dioxide and sulphate in the air as the rest of northern Scandinavia, despite the fact that there are no local causes of pollution on the island. The industrial fallout can be traced to both northern U.S.S.R. and to Europe. Even dust from the Gobi and Sahara deserts can be found at an altitude of 4,000 metres (13,000 feet).

Norway has the supremacy on Svalbard, and this is on the whole respected by the signatories to the Svalbard Treaty, although in these northern waters open to European Community fishing vessels, situations somewhat reminiscent of a 'cod war' can arise.

The Barents Sea is the area where Norway faces her most important challenge in foreign policy. Despite the negotiations on fishing boundaries that have been carried on between Norway and the Soviet Union since 1974, they have not yet been able to agree. Nor have the two countries reached accord on how the continental shelf should be divided up between them.

It can hardly be any easier for Norway to hold on to her possessions on the far side of the world, in the Antarctic. Norwegians are usually proud of the fact that they have never had colonies, or at least have only penguins and walrusses as their subjects. In fact, the country lays claim to Bouvet Island, Peter I's Land and Queen Maud Land, the last an icy waste seven times the size of Norway. However, the ice cap, which is up to 3,000 metres (10,000 feet) thick, could conceal valuable metals.

Norwegians have always had an indomitable urge to ski to the South Pole. Roald Amundsen was the first to get there on 14 December 1911. After that, we busied ourselves hunting whales and annexing territories in the Antarctic. Peter I's Land was seen for the first time by the Russian Bellinghause expedition in 1821, and was given the name of the czar. Yet it was the whaling captain Nils Larsen who went ashore in 1929 and planted the Norwegian flag there. Two years previously the Norwegians had laid claim to Bouvet Island. In 1939 Queen Maud Land was formally taken over.

The only snag about these territories, some 15,000 kilometres

162. The town of Lillehammer, some 200 kilometres (125 miles) north of Oslo, is a centre of the arts and tourism, and a busy town all year round. It is the venue of the Winter Olympic Games of 1994. (Pål Hermansen/Samfoto/NN)

(nearly 10,000 miles) away from the Norwegian Parliament, is that no other countries recognize our right to them, or that of any other state claiming to own land in the Antarctic. The vast continent is divided up like a cake between Australia, Great Britain, Argentina, Chile, New Zealand, France and Norway. According to the terms of the Antarctic Treaty that came into effect in 1961, it is impossible for any country to lay claims to the area, carry out any form of military activity, conduct nuclear tests or dump nuclear waste there.

Enough about our foreign policy!

I will not deny that there are things that preoccupy Norwegians more than the Antarctic in their relationship to the rest of the world. There are, for instance, many of us who worry about what will happen to Norwegian culture under the massive Anglo-American influence that is swamping us. The most pessimistic predict that the Norwegian language will not survive for more than thirty years under the impact.

Medieval convent seal.

Norwegians have always gathered ideas from the rest of the world. Just look at Norwegian architecture! The solid, traditional timbered houses that you can still see in the valleys, and in places like the Norwegian Folk Museum in Oslo and Maihaugen in Lillehammer, have been giving way to one international style after another. The small houses along the coast are the result of century-long contact across the North Sea with England and the Netherlands, but have been adapted to Norwegian reality by our master builders, whose skills were formed by wind and weather. Round the turn of the century came the Swiss chalet style with dragon heads and carving, later to be supplanted by its very opposite, severe and rectangular functionalism, *funkis* as it is called in Norway. Today Post-Modernism has softened the lines of large buildings with cheerful colours and a free mixing of styles.

Housing estates get more and more similar: three-quarters of all newly built small houses consist of boring, prefabricated square units, constructed on the drawing board by the manufacturers, delivered ready to be placed on their foundations and painted in the colours of the year by Ola and Kari and their friends.

We have always lived on the outskirts of Europe. While the Swedes got their first university in 1477, and the Danes in 1479, we did not get ours until 1811. While our neighbours with their royal courts could look back on centuries of theatre, opera and ballet, we had to wait for our own national theatre until 1899. We got our national opera in 1958 (with no opera house), and our college of music in 1973.

Our only painter who is truly internationally known, Edvard Munch, had to go to Germany to gain recognition before he was acknowledged at home. Our great dramatist, Henrik Ibsen, had to seek refuge in the south of Europe for twenty-seven years because this mountain country was too narrow for him. And our great composer, Edvard Grieg, had to study in Germany before he could write his famous and truly Norwegian Concerto in A-minor, composed in Denmark. In after times we honour them with museums!

Right up to our day many Norwegian artists have had to go abroad to study. In particular we have exported singers; Kirsten Flagstad, Ingrid Bjoner and Aase Nordmo Løvberg are well-known names in the opera world. Jazz musicians like singer Karin Krog and tenor saxophonist Jan Garbarek have won international fame through festivals and recordings, even if they have stayed at home. The Oslo Philharmonic Orchestra under the Soviet conductor Mariss Jansons and the Norwegian Chamber rchestra under the Briton Iona Brown have also received international claim. The painter and sculptor Kjell Erik Killi Olsen, sculptor Bard reivik, and textile artist Jan Groth are making a name for themselves broad.

There is no particular wish to isolate ourselves. We translate a mass foreign literature, and we cultivate our international connections rough the Bergen festivals, the festival of church music in Kristiansand, e jazz festivals in Kongsberg and Molde, and the graphics festival in redrikstad. But after the experience of being subjected to foreign owers for centuries, it is natural that we would like to have a say when ur fate is to be decided — as we had in 1972 when we said 'no' to the EC. Yet the traditional Norwegian sense of inferiority combined with an creasing lack of historical awareness has brought out an abject and ncritical admiration of all things American, especially in the tabloid ress. This cultural state of puberty in a young and uncertain nation has iven free rein to the commercial pop industry. A random list of the eek's top-selling LP's printed in the Oslo paper *Dagbladet* one winter's ay could produce only six titles in Norwegian and four in Swedish out of 0 albums. The rest were Anglo-American. French and German pop usic is rarely heard in Norway. Very few rock groups sing in Norwe- ian, for if one is to make one's way in the world, like 'A-Ha', it has to be English.

The traditional Norwegian national instrument, the harding fiddle, an hardly compete against this pressure, despite its beautiful, but omplicated music, full of ornaments and embellishments. Our contem- orary composers have fared better, and Arne Nordheim and the Italian- orn Antonio Bibalo are continually having their great dramatic works or allets performed abroad. Our senior composer, Harald Sæverud of ergen, is more popular than ever. Thanks to state subsidies, most of our ontemporary music is accessible on LP records.

The State has recognized the consequences of the fact that Norway a small and exposed linguistic area, and has taken measures to ensure e country keeps its scattered population, its language and its culture. ost-war cultural policy has been to send on tour films, paintings and culpture, theatre and music, to all corners of the country. The state-run ural cinema used to visit 1,000 small places a year in its heyday, before e arrival of the video. The touring theatre, Riksteatret, and the travel- ng art gallery went all over the country, the state concert society rganized both local concerts and tours. Each district had its own library, nd even the district of Oslo sent round a book bus. People not only orrow books; the commercial publishers' own book club became a roar- ng success, selling 48 million books in the course of its first 25 years - 30 to each Norwegian home!

From the 70s the cultural policy has been one of decentralization nd democratization. Regional theatres have been set up in many towns, nd there are arts centres run by the artists themselves. The govern- ment has introduced grants, and 485 artists received guaranteed ncomes in 1987. To support writers, the State buys 1,000 copies of all ew Norwegian works of fiction, which it distributes among the libraries f the country.

Foreigners probably know Norwegian literature best through the vorks of Henrik Ibsen and Knut Hamsun, Trygve Gulbranssen and Agnar Mykle. The children's authors Alf Prøysen, Thorbjørn Egner and Anne- Cath Vestly also have readers all over the word.

Of the 2,500 books published yearly in Norway, 300 are works of fiction. The most translated among recent prose writers are Knut Faldbakken, Vera Henriksen, Bjørg Vik and Herbjørg Wassmo. Olav H. Hauge, Rolf Jacobsen and Jan Erik Vold are reckoned as the most important poets today.

Kari and Ola Nordmann also read magazines, journals and, of course, newspapers. There are some 160 newspapers with a circulation of 3.2 million in this country with only 1.5 million households. There is some measure of state support to sustain such a varied press. The state broadcasting company, Norsk Rikskringkasting, had a monopoly on radio and TV transmissions in the country until the 1980s. Since then the air has been free for all.

It may not strengthen us culturally that our small country has two official languages of equal standing, in addition to the less prestigious Såmi. In the Viking days we all spoke Old Norse, much as they do in Iceland today. Then the Danes forced their language on us through four centuries of supremacy. This Danish/Norwegian is our main language today. It has become more Norwegian in time, losing much of the pomposity of the old administrative ruling class, but it has never absorbed the smile that is to be found in modern Danish. The other language, New Norwegian, built up from our dialects and formed by Ivar Aasen in the nineteenth century, is richer and more melodious. Many of our greatest writers have used New Norwegian, including Olav Duun and Tarjei Vesaas, who have perhaps been the most European of us all. Citizens can demand official forms written in the language of their choice. Norsk Rikskringkasting is obliged to put out 25 per cent of its programmes in New Norwegian. Of the 454 local authorities in the country, 114 (with a population of 500,000) have chosen New Norwegian as their official language, 181 (with 1.6 million) have chosen Danish/Norwegian, while 159 (with 2 million) remain neutral.

The two languages are very similar, and the official language policy in our century has been to amalgamate them into one common laguage. This has aroused a long and bitter language dispute that is still going on. Today the opponents ought really to bury the hatchet and join forces in the battle against Americanization and other foreign influences. This has already had some bizarre consequences: the laundry or *vaskeri* has turned into a *vaskoteque*, while the barber's shop has become a *klippoteque*. Whatever next?

Perhaps more Norwegian than anything else is the earth closet or outdoor latrine, that small house with a heart carved in the door and the coronation portrait from Trondheim in 1906 on the wall. Whether it is a two-seater or a six-man privy with a small seat for the children, the thunderbox has been literally the seat of Ola Nordmann's growth and development. Here he could sit in peace and quiet while snowstorms howled or bees hummed in the bluebells. This has been his spiritual home, this is where he worked out his philosophy. Today the outdoor privy is on its way out. It has had its own book written, and it has its own fan club, *Gammeldassens venner* (Friends of the Old Loo). It won't be long before it becomes an antique. One thing is certain though: it will be a black day for Norwegian culture when the tourist officers try to attract their customers with a *shitoteque*. Though you never know!

In the mid-1980s the state-owned Norwegian oil company Statoil sent a letter to Norway's Fishermen's Union in English. The sturdy fishermen accepted the challenge, and answered – in Old Norse!

Important Dates

8000 BC	Earliest traces of Stone Age hunters and fishermen, and rock carvings.
00–2500 BC	Farming peoples settle in east Norway.
00–500 BC	Bronze Age.
0 BC	Iron Age begins.
d c AD	Earliest runic inscriptions.
h–7th c	Migrations and unquiet times, hill forts for defence.
h c	Small clan-based states with judicial assemblies develop.
00–1050	The Viking Age. Settlements founded in Ireland, Great Britain, France, Iceland, Greenland and northern isles. Voyages to Vinland (North American cons to Vinland (North American coast). Plundering raids in the Mediterranean.
900	Development of regional courts of law based on the representative system, and a defence system based on the people's duty to build, maintain and man ships.
900	King Harald I Fairhaired unites much of Norway.
5–1000	Reign of Olaf I Tryggvason, who forcibly converts his subjects to Christianity. He dies in battle against King Sweyn I of Denmark.
015–30	Reign of Olaf II Haraldsson, first king of all Norway. By force and with the help of Anglo-Saxon missionaries he completes the conversion of his people. After his death in battle against Norwegian allies of Canute, king of Denmark and England, he is sanctified as St Olaf.
66	Harald III Hardraade (Hardruler) invades northern England and is killed at Stamford Bridge in battle against King Harold Godwinson of England, three days before the landing of William of Normandy near Hastings.
52	Archbishopric is founded at Nidaros (Trondheim), where a great cathedral is built.
2th and 3th c	Great social changes. Rapid growth of population, and rise of secular and clerical aristocracy. Freeholders become tenants.
130–1240	Civil wars.
217–63	Reign of Haakon IV Haakonsson, who establishes a strong and united kingdom after a century of civil wars. Royal administration and control of Norwegian settlements strengthened. Trade flourishes with the settlement of German merchants in Bergen and elsewhere.
263–80	Reign of Magnus V Lagabøter (Lawmender), who creates a national code of laws.
349	The Black Death kills one to two thirds of the population, thus devastating the economy and weakening the state.

Typical examples of Viking craftsmanship in fashioning gold jewelry.

Caricature of Henrik Ibsen, Norway's most celebrated writer.

1397	Union with Denmark and Sweden under Eric of Pomerania following the death of Olaf IV (1387), last of the old royal line
1442	Christopher III of Denmark accepted as Norwegian king. Danish monarchs henceforth rule the country until 1814.
1536	Norwegians accept the Reformation (Evangelical Lutheran Church).
1588–1648	Reign of Christian IV, who rebuilds Oslo (Christiania) after a great fire. Rapid development of mining and lumber mills.
1660	The king gains absolute power.
1811	Foundation of Oslo University in the reign of Frederick VI.
1807–1814	Denmark-Norway take part in the Napoleonic wars as French allies. Blockade and famine in Norway.
1814	Denmark cedes Norway to Sweden. Norwegians declare themselves independent. A national assembly works out a democratic constitution. Norway is forced to accept union with Sweden under the Swedish crown, but retains its own constitution and parliament. Civil servants form the dominant class in society.
1840s	Ivar Aasen creates the New Norwegian written language (Nynorsk) on the basis of dialects. Henrik Wergeland (1808–1845), poet and social reformer, writes his finest lyrical poetry. National romanticism strongly influences art and literature. Decade of social reforms.
1863	Birth of Edvard Munch (d. 1944), Norway's greatest painter and graphic artist.
1866/67	Henrik Ibsen (1828–1906) publishes *Brand* and *Peer Gynt,* the first of his major plays.
1868	Edvard Grieg (1843–1907) composes his famous Piano Concerto.
1884	The parliamentary system strengthens the power of the Storting (Parliament).
1898	Universal male suffrage.
1905	Union with Sweden dissolved by decision of the Storting and a national plebiscite. A second plebiscite is four to one in favour of a monarchy over a republic. Prince Charles (Carl) of Denmark becomes king as Haakon VII.
1913	Female suffrage.
1914–18	Norway remains neutral in World War I, but her shipping aids Great Britain.
1919–1927	Alcohol prohibition.
1920	Norwegian sovreignty over Svalbard recognized.
1935	First Labour government.
1940	German invasion (April 9). King Haakon and government move to London. Vidkun Quisling installed as 'minister president' (1942) and Josef Terboven as 'Reichskommissar'.
1945	Norway liberated (May). Labour Party returned to power in general election.
1945–1965	Labour Party in power.
1949	Norway joins NATO.
1957–91	Reign of Oaf V.
1960	Norway a founder member of the European Free Trade Association (EFTA).
1965–1971	Non-socialist coalition government.
1971	First oil well starts production in the Ekofisk field.
1972	Referendum rejects membership of the Common Market (EEC).
1981	First woman prime minister, Gro Harlem Brundtland, heads Labour government.
1991	Harald V ascends the throne.

Photographs:

B. AREKLETT/SAMFOTO/NN (77)

O. ÅSHEIM/SAMFOTO (41, 121)

HANS HVIDE BANG/SAMFOTO/NN (7, 8, 89, 97, 104, 109)

HANS HVIDE BANG/SAMFOTO (95, 100)

JØRN BØHMER OLSEN, R. SØRENSEN/NN (96)

T. BØLSTAD/SAMFOTO (43)

JOHAN BRUN/NN (60, 135, 136)

SVEIN-ERIK DAHL/SAMFOTO (22, 23, 118, 157, 158, 159)

O. D. ENERSEN/SAMFOTO/NN (74, 76)

ROGER ENGVIK (119, 123)

KNUT ENSTAD (20)

BETTEN FOSSE/SAMFOTO (116)

F. FRIBERG/NN (61)

RAGNAR FRISLID/NN (49, 64, 75, 90–92, 98, 101, 102, 106, 111, 127, 134, 141, 143, 144, 146, 148–156, 160, 161)

A. O. GAUTESTAD/NN (68)

KIM HART/SAMFOTO (26, 41, 72)

HUGO HENRIKSEN/SAMFOTO (88)

PÅL HERMANSEN/SAMFOTO/NN (10, 59, 99, 103, 122, 124–126, 128–130, 142, 162)

HUSMO-FOTO (1–5, 11, 12, 14, 18, 19, 21, 24, 25, 28–34, 36, 38, 45, 47, 48, 50–54, 56, 57, 63, 65, 71, 80–85, 87, 93, 94, 107, 108, 113, 133, 138, 139, 140, 147)

DAG KJELSAAS/NN/SAMFOTO (66)

KNUDSENS FOTOSENTER (69)

R. LISLERUD/SAMFOTO (40)

M. LØBERG/SAMFOTO (44, 112)

M. LØBERG/SAMFOTO/NN (13)

MITTET (15–17, 46, 58, 62, 114, 120, 131)

A. NORMANN/SAMFOTO (145)

OLA RØE/SAMFOTO (78)

PER-ANDERS ROSENKVIST/SAMFOTO (115)

ROLF SØRENSEN/NN/SAMFOTO (67)

HELGE SUNDE (6, 35, 37, 39, 55, 86, 117)

HELGE SUNDE/SAMFOTO (27, 73, 79, 137)

TORE WUTTUDAL/NN/SAMFOTO (70)

Index